Contents

Preface

BEING A PROFESSIONAL WRITER
A Guide to Good Practice

STEPHEN WADE
&
KATE WALKER

Emerald Publishing
www.emeraldpublishing.co.uk

British Cataloguing in Publication data. A catalogue record is available for this book from the British Library.

ISBN 184716045X
ISBN 13: 9781847160454

Printed in the United Kingdom by Biddles Ltd Kings Lynn Norfolk

Cover Design by Bookworks Islington

Whilst every effort has been made to ensure that the information in this book is accurate at the time of going to print, the author and publisher recognise that the information can become out of date. The book is therefore sold on the understanding that no responsibility for errors and omissions is assumed and no responsibility is held for the information held within.

Preface

There are plenty of handbooks available introducing the craft of creative writing. What makes this one different? Mainly, I have made sure that the material here is up-dated and current. The book is meant to lead you steadily into writing as a craft as well as an art. The first short exercises and basic advice may be useful for complete beginners, or they may also help practising writers to 'take stock'.

We have taught creative writing for almost thirty years, and in that time have learned that genuine writing is honest, from some creative centre we have, with a strong aim to share, express and communicate the human situation. That will be a constant, whether you want to write freelance articles or epic novels. Everything that is going to be genuine, your true writer's voice, will germinate in that unique creative centre.

The chapters here deal with the basics of all creative writing, and also introduce some of the most popular forms and categories. It is not possible to cover all the genres here, but my second book, building on this, is *Keep on Writing Professionally,* and this focuses on the professional practice skills and issues such as contracts, copyright and editorial or publishing procedures.

But *Getting Started as a Professional Writer* takes you from short warm-up exercises to research and drafting of full-length works. We have to thank Graham Mort, Roger McGough, Suzanne Ruthven and all our former writing students for helping to bring out much of the groundwork of this book.

Stephen Wade and Kate Walker

1

You the Writer

One-minute summary – There are as many writing 'voices' as there are writers.

Research has shown that we each have a specific way of using language, and that the old rule about 'Don't write the way you speak' is not necessarily the right advice.

Successful writing is defined as that variety of verbal composition that you personally wish to produce. Therefore it is virtually impossible simply to produce that writing to a satisfactory level without preparation. This pre-writing stage is the subject of the first chapter. We look at established ways of using your own resources and life-experience; then we move on to a consideration of the choices open to you in forms, conventions and genres.

In this chapter you will learn:
- How to access and use your own resources and experience
- What thinking goes into choosing your writing category
- How to take stock of yourself as a reader and writer
- What factors influence your decisions: long-term planning and aims

Taking stock of experience

Write from life?

In our lives as writers, from the first sentences at school to the writing of an epic novel, we tend to play safe most of the time and 'write about what we know', but no-one is sure whether or not we fall into two groups of those who write from actuality

7

and those who have to make things up. For many of us, telling stories is a mixture of both. But some of us feel safer and more comfortable with 'facts'. Some experience is ideal for use in creative writing and some has very little potential. But these definitions change with every individual.

Is everything a fit subject for writing?

In 1925, a writer on literature said that there were five subjects for poetry: love, nature, women, life and religious belief. What he meant by 'life' is unclear, but it is true that in the period of English history up to the early twentieth century there were certain subjects considered to be suitable for poetry and some that were not.

We live in different times. The pace of life has accelerated and the communications revolution has meant that the global village concept has changed our ideas about the personal life. To take stock of one single life – to log and comment on a constant flow of life-data – has become the focal concern of modern writers. Therefore, in starting out as a writer, consider some fundamental ideas about your life and how it is or is not 'material' for your writing.

For instance, think about these questions:
Do you find it easy to invent stories and characters?
In conversation, are you mainly a talker or a listener?
Do you always have the habit of reflecting on your life (as in a diary)?
When you choose a book to read for pleasure, do you like imagined worlds or a world that reflect the real world?

A matter of taste

Taking stock of experience, with potential creative writing in mind, is largely about considering yourself in ways you perhaps never did before. These questions are meant to make you think about your instinctive relationship with books and stories, words and life itself.

There are many ways to examine your life, and the maxim from Socrates that to 'know thyself' is the basis of wisdom applies here too. In writing classes there are always plenty of people who have never undergone this initial thinking stage, and they start to write without a foundation of real knowledge.

In doing the following preparatory exercises, always follow your 'taste' in art and storytelling. The word for the study of beauty and art, aesthetics, is useful here. Each of us has an aesthetic profile and this plays a major part in our formation as artists and writers. For instance, you could list these:

Favourite stories – in any genre?
Preferences in 'highbrow' and 'lowbrow' literature and art?
Music and the visual arts in your life – decoration and time-filling only?
Time spent discussing art, books and ideas?

A recent debate in the media looked yet again at the question of 'Is Bob Dylan a better poet than John Keats?' This is a meaningless question, though it has its interest for a writer. The word 'better' has no meaning. As Shakespeare said, 'What is ought but as 'tis valued?' In other words, you like what you like: end of story. But as an aspiring writer you need to know where you stand in terms of this aesthetic profile. That means being sure of your answers to questions like these:

➤ What kinds of stories interest you most and why?
➤ Do you make time to talk about responses to these stories?
➤ Do you tend to feel deep responses to art, with no need to talk?
➤ Have you dismissed some art-forms from life – and why?

> ➤ Why do you dismiss stories told in particular forms and genres?

> ➤ For example, if people mention jazz or opera or modern dance, do you immediately 'turn off'? Do you only like 'what you like' or are you open to new aesthetic ideas and forms?

Life and art: transmutation

All these questions are important because people tend to form their tastes without reason or purpose. There may be no pattern. But if you have favourite book that you always return to, then start relating this to your own use of words and love of stories. Our lives are our most profound and probably infinite resource when we start to write. The ordinary life is often overlooked. Never discount experience, and never say that nothing worth writing about has ever happened to you. Gustave Flaubert set out to write his story *a Simple Heart* as a challenge: to make an ordinary life extraordinarily interesting.

Creative writing of any kind is about taking a second look, or even dredging feelings and responses from life-date that have long passed into the 'dark backward and abysm of time.' Writing is about reclamation – but of feelings, not fossils from rock.

Aims and aspirations

Why are you writing?

We all have different reasons for wanting to write. For some it may be a personal ambition simply to see their name in print. Others may want to change the world. P.G. Wodehouse quite clearly invented Jeeves and Wooster to entertain. Although critics have read all kinds of meanings into the books, the intention of the writer is always almost impossible to pin down. John Braine, author of *Room at the Top*, was once asked how hard it was writing a scathing indictment of corruption in regional British political life. He replied that he just wanted to write a story of love and desire.

For the writer setting out in any type of composition, from screen-writing to science fiction, the question needs answering at the early sage: for whom do you write?

The old man and the poor woman

A famous American novelist once expressed this point in this way. He said we should decide whether we want to write for the rich old man, in a wheelchair with a butler by him and a rug over his knees, reading your paragraph over a third time, or for the young woman in the tenement, desperately trying to finish her romance novel before the candle goes out, as she has no coins for the meter. So, for whom do you write?

Give some thought to your own specific aims in writing. You might consider these factors:

➢ Is there a writer who is your 'template' or role model? (Why?)
➢ Do you want to entertain or instruct the reader – or both?
➢ Is the research and preparation as interesting to you as the writing itself?
➢ Have you been told by friends/parents/teachers that you can writer particular things?

Stages of Writing

In our lives as writers, after we have mastered basic sentence structure and can produce fluent prose with suitable vocabulary, we tend to go through six stages:

One: releasing

Here we write largely for ourselves. The nature of this writing is a need to put feelings into words to make sense of them, and to express responses to experience. There is no sense of readership.

Two: documenting-limited

Here we are still coping with the factual basis of writing, although a readership may be intended.

Three: documenting extended

Choices are now being made about the form and expression of the material gathered. For instance, something may take the form of a short story, a one-act play or an article.

Four: narrating-limited

Now we make new and hesitant efforts to use forms and conventions which have a defined reader. So this could be our first writing in genre or in-house style.

Five: narrating-extended

There is now a more profound understanding of the shared experience of the text by reader and writer. So this is very advanced, with a sure sense of the right style and language needed.

Six: critiquing

The final stage is that at which we can apply long and insightful reflection on the texts we have produced: so detailed editing, re-writing and drafting are part of this, but also the placing of our writing within a wide context of writing in society generally.

These terms come from research done by Dr Greg Light, and full details of his writing are included in the bibliography. Notice that the process is one that starts with a simple unloading of experience (otherwise often called *catharsis*) and progresses eventually to a full understanding of the writing process, at which we can stand back and see the work in context.

Choice of forms and genres

One of the most exciting aspects of the writing scene today is that genres have melted and mixed in exciting ways. A genre is a term used for a defined category of writing; for instance, science fiction, western, detective story, documentary – these are all terms used to describe specific genres. This naming of parts helps writers to decide what they want to do. But in the last twenty years everything has blurred. In c. 1900 it was clear what kind of read one could expect if one picked up a mystery story. A biography then would have been factual, well-researched and safely chronological.

Now it is different. Julian Barnes's novel, *Flaubert's Parrot*, for instance, published in 1989, is technically a 'novel' but is also at the same time a work of biography and a handbook on writing. New 'genre cocktails' have come along with names like cyberpunk, inner space science fiction or western romance. Typical of this is the use of the term 'creative non-fiction' and this comprises a range of genres such as travel writing, memoir, confession, autobiography and reportage. In summary, all this is to your advantage. You need not worry too much in the sense of *literary* descriptions of genres. What matters more if you write for publication is the *publisher's* concept of a genre.

If you like….

This point is all about the ways in which a publisher likes to sell books, but also relates to the writer's aspirations. In other words, in many publishers' catalogues, you will find a sentence like:

'If you loved Stephen King's Carrie then you'll adore this new book by Joe Bloggs….'

In the film *The Player* Tim Robbins sits at his desk in Hollywood and listens to writers pitching ideas all day. They sit in front of him and say that their story is *'King Kong* meets *Die Hard* and so on. He has his own notions of popularity and successful mixes of genre.

Go your own way?

This leads us to a summary of two ways of working when starting out in creative writing. First, you might be the sort of writer who puts everything on paper very quickly, in a mess, and then re-writes. Or second, you might be a careful planner who has to write from copious notes, very steadily and clearly. The point is to do whatever works for you. There are no right and wrong ways to go about it. Roald Dahl liked a quiet garden shed and lots of small rituals. Jack Kerouac wrote straight from the head, and at great length. Josephine Hart, author of *Damage*, once said that she 'starts small and goes smaller'.

I can suggest four types of writer in this context:

The Liberator

This writer lets all the words go their own way. Shaping and changing can come later with the wonders of word-processing.

The Controller

This writer has to have every sentence ready to slot into the precise place, for the right effect. Lots of notes are written before writing.

The Impressionist

This writer jots down the 'spine' of the text, in any order, but in a minimal form, to be filled out later.

The Strategist

This writer treats a text as a bundle of different styles and voices, all to be integrated according to a pattern. Hence, some people want every page to have at least four lines of dialogue!

Reading and writing

Now is the time to ask the crucial questions relating to the proposition that the reader you are makes the writer that you will become. There is no doubt that there is a strong link between the fiction we read and the fiction we want to write. If non-fiction is your preference, then ask yourself what subjects or types of knowledge you have always been drawn to. But in some ways a body of knowledge markedly different from the writing you do is desirable. Several successful poets have found that the substance of their work relates to a body of knowledge in a particular area: in Seamus Heaney's work, ancient and medieval history play a large part; in Ted Hughes' poetry his knowledge of anthropology and natural history was always evident.

But at the beginning of your career in creative writing, it is well worth understanding why and what you read on a regular basis. Key topics here are:

The way you choose reading:

Do you try anything within certain categories or do you purposely look for books that push the boundaries of the genre? Have you subconsciously homed in on a sub-genre? For instance, some writers are crime writers but only write one version of the genre, having read only one version. Think about the sub-genres in crime fiction:

Detective
Who-done-it
Psychological
Thriller

Historical crime and so on

Then there is the way you read. As you read this and hopefully start your writing life fully, make a note of the methods you can employ to maximise the benefits of your directed and purposeful reading:

1. *Read for technique* rather than the central story.
   Take a favourite book in your category. Read a few chapters purely to note the effects, tricks of style and small details that make it work for you.

2. *Copy key passages* or images into a personal anthology notebook.

3. *Read the character details* from three books in your genre. Actually copy and note the different methods of character-writing employed.

Tutorial
Progress questions

1. What is to be gained from listing three most important reasons for wanting to write.
2. Have you ever written for 'catharsis' purposes?
3. Why does writing tend to be very individual in the first stage of writing?

Discussion points

In the discussion points in this book, the purpose is to give you material for reflection in your writer's notebook.

1.   Why would a writer choose to write without any attention to a defined genre?
2.   What is to be gained by deciding on a special area of writing early on in a career?

Practical assignments

1.   Look up some accounts of starting to write in writers' autobiographies or in interviews with successful writers. What tends to be the most common advice and why?
2.   Taking Greg Light's terms for the stages of writing, compare a piece of fiction by a beginner with that of an established 'name' and try to detect differences.
3.   Look up George Orwell's essay called *Why I write* (see bibliography) and see where you agree or disagree with his reasons.
4. Find an article about learning/teaching creative writing, such as the one by David Lodge (see bibliography) and include your own thoughts on what can be taught/learned in your notebook.

Study tip

1.   Collect any statements about learning to write written by established writers and find common ground in what they say. For instance, there is the factor X of ideas coming from

no identified source, and the point made once by Jack Higgins "Sometimes I can be just staring out of the window in the study...and   that's part of working..."

2.	Look at my categories of writer. Which are you? Look at some of your writing from schoolwork and see if you can find that aspect of your writing early on in your life.

****

2

Observation and recording

One-minute summary – Now that most of the fundamental points about aims and foundation thinking have been made, the next stage is to look at cultivating the first stages of writing and moving from functional to creative generation of words, phrases and notes. Of course, as we look at the basis of effective writing, there is the whole area of grammar and syntax to look at, but that is not our primary interest here. The concepts dealt with in this chapter are voice, tone and style – all hard to define but we know they are working well when work is read aloud. The other sections here deal with the disciplines of monitoring ideas, building up powers of writing through observation, and keeping a well-conceived personal anthology. Above all, this chapter is concerned with organisation and directed thinking.

In this chapter, you will learn:
➢ How to develop creative ideas through writing prose passages in a notebook.
➢ How to access your own words and ideas for writing by methodical planning.

The basis of good writing
This might seem easy. People too easily define 'good writing' by means of the apparent evidence that the writer knows 'rules' of grammar and spelling. But most creative writers will tell you that all grammars melt. That is, knowing the rules of correct expression is necessary, but in creativity, rules are there to be broken. Good writing in the sense used in this context means writing that meets the criteria set by the writer (or

editor/publisher as you go on in writing). Simple practices like reading aloud or asking for feedback from friends are common ways to tell when a piece 'feels' right. But in another sense, the question 'When is a piece of writing finished?' is a tough one. Many famous poets, for example, kept on revising poems for years, well after the work had first appeared in print. Sometimes poems are axed from a poet's corpus of work because time brings with it a sense of dissatisfaction.

A sense of authenticity

First attempts at writing creatively need a bedrock of authentic feeling. Behind this is the ongoing problem of saying exactly what you mean: every writer knows that there is a pre-verbal stage: the point at which the thing you want to write is merely something vaguely in the mind. Then the whole process of transmuting a feeling or a thought into a structure of words, phrases, sentences and paragraphs begins and the feeling of the original impulse ebbs away.

This has to be approached sensibly, with an acceptance that what you will have on paper is a compromise, but you work hard to come as near as you possibly can to what you hope will be there. The main enemy of being authentic and developing an authentic voice is the sense of 'being a writer'. Someone once described this as 'standing on tip-toe' for effect. This is what happens (in a simplified way).

Stage 1   You have the clear idea of what the writing will be.

Stage 2   You start to write and a point comes at which it runs away from you: what you wanted eludes you. You work hard to return to the first Impulse behind the 'voice' of the piece.

Stage 3   The editing and drafting begins. You re-write carefully.

Stage 4   You accept the best you can do.

How do you avoid the posture, the mind-set of 'being a writer' and simply write what you feel, while at the same time adding style? The wisest course seems to be to start writing by working on the pulse behind effective prose. A useful example of this is to build up descriptions of everyday things. This involves looking with fresh eyes at what is familiar. The pattern might be something like this:

Topic: Looking out of the window

The garden is full of summer. Everything seems to be the greenest it can be, or yellow as yellow can ever reach for.

You have the central thought. Now add to this by following the theme of extremes and excess:

There is something exciting about seeing and hearing all that life. Just a short walk to the far end brings a hundred different sounds and smells. Early August, and there are wall browns busy around the straggling buddleia.

This has kept to the same voice and subject. The prose has a rhythm, a pulse running through it. Writing has to start with this, rather than with a purely syntactical basis. If the voice is authentic, the punctuation, word order and vocabulary will follow almost naturally. Although later editing will always be needed.

Using a Notebook

A thorough search of the literature shelves at a good reference or university library will reveal just how much printed material is available about creative writing in a secondary capacity. These are ancillary texts; for example, a line of books on Keats might have these:

The poetical work themselves
Biographical studies
Critical works
Secondary works by the author: letters, notebooks, drafts etc.

Not every famous writer kept notebooks; many kept them but never intended them for publication. For the present purpose, I'm suggesting that you find some in print and learn what the value of meticulous notebook entries can be. Notable examples of writers whose notebooks are easily available in print are Dylan Thomas, G.M. Hopkins, Allan Ginsberg and C.K.Williams. ~There are many more, but these are well known. Why are they so useful and how does a writer keep control of them?

Never losing an idea

For most writers, the first value of a notebook is that it is constantly with them and they write down the germ of a potential writing subject as soon as an observation takes place. This is a typical example from my own poetry notebook (I have books for poetry, fiction and factual writing):

Overheard two senior citizens in the café today expressing concern about crime. They were dour Yorkshire, clothed in grey or fawn, and happy to lament and grumble. It seemed to be their only way of conversing. Typical statements were: 'It'll be shut within twelve week.' And 'I see Blair's dropped another clanger.'

Notice that this is partly aural (I listened) and partly visual (I looked). I wrote the note as I sat in the busy café in between reading. As a fiction writer, I never avoid listening to actual conversation. It's the only way to cultivate an 'ear' for authentic dialogue.

Sometimes the note is simply an image, like the time I saw a gathering of birds on some telegraph wires and immediately was reminded of musical notes on a stave. For most writers, notebooks are for scraps like this. Christopher Isherwood, writing of his friend, W H Auden, said:

"...Auden developed a severe attack of allusions, jargon and private jokes.

He began to write lines like *inexorable Rembrandt rays that stab*.. Nearly all the poems of that early Eliot period are scrapped..."

Isherwood saw that Auden's notebooks were part of a learning curve. He was trying out his ideas and seeing what he could do. This would be good advice for anyone starting to write.

Observation: a second look

Writing notebooks are excellent for trying out style and new ways of approaching your subjects. A useful guideline when beginning is to have an organising principle for your notebook or notebooks. You might arrange things like this:

Notebook for Style

In this you put together scraps of ideas that may have emerged throughout the day or week. You can build up paragraphs and short articles or stories in this way.

Notebook for observation

This is the heart of the matter: practise writing about ordinary things in such a way that they are made new, made vivid and different, through your pen.

For instance, think how difficult it is to describe a nose. You could rely on accepted visual words like retroussé or 'Roman' or 'hook' but is it possible to convey an individual nose as well as a painter like Reynolds or Van Gogh could? We may not think so, but we can keep working at it.

Using templates

Another worthwhile purpose for notebooks is to write short pieces of poetry or prose from 'template' texts. That is, you copy the style, voice or metre of the original, just to try out your ability with language. This was a common learning method in the eighteenth century, when writers learned poetry by a process of 'imitation'. What you are doing is a kind of translation, turning one text into another, making it your own. The form of a parody is a simple way of practising skills. You might try a poetic form, or a type of very distinctive prose.

A simple way to do this is to take an author who has a very distinctive prose style – say Conan Doyle's Sherlock Holmes stories or Raymond Chandler's hard-boiled Philip Marlowe stories. Read an opening page or a typical passage several times, then write from memory, trying to copy the 'voice' of the text.

You could even produce a 'genre cocktail' by mixing two of these for fun, and for extending yourself. The point of all this is to see what constitutes an individual voice. Raymond Chandler's has these features:

A powerful use of similes
Short, laconic statements
A tone of ironic or sarcastic disenchantment with the 'world' of the novel
A vocabulary mixing romance with disillusion and seediness.

Speaking and writing

The real importance of all this logging of ideas and practising style is to pinpoint the importance of your own natural speaking voice. The question is: how much of your innate personality actually filters into your writing style? People often think that innovating the words, by being an expert on language, is the way to be a good writer – to be original. But perhaps we need to keep developing ourselves? Somerset Maugham said that we need to constantly enlarge and examine our own perceptions in order to be original and startlingly interesting in what we write.

An interesting way to consider the rift between how we speak and how we write is to record oneself reading a passage of fiction. When played back the recording soon highlights your intonation and pitch. Logically, our sense of how we read a piece of prose will tell us something about how we write the same.

The idea of a commonplace book

A similar idea, but for a different purpose, is the use of a commonplace book. This is a basis for the factual, authentic basis of whatever you choose to write. It has been said that readers' imaginations have a 'feeling for fact'. We all love to have a sense of an actual, understood world for the setting of a novel, or even a desire for factual details in a non-fiction book. Therefore, a writer needs a method of logging the *research* basis of writing, in addition to the purely *verbal* basis. Consider the different reasons why you may need research before writing:

➢ Verification of place, topography, social context etc.
➢ Accuracy of speech in the period of the setting or the social context.
➢ Crucial facts such as dates and places to define a period or a mental milieu.
➢ Small detail for characters such as clothing, vocabulary, education.

A perfect example is in the historical fiction of Bernard Cornwell, creator of Captain Sharpe in the Peninsular War novels. Cornwell has to make Sharpe live in our minds but his imagination and sense of empathy with his creation can only go so far. He also needs to be informed about the types of rifle used in 1806, what the uniform of a sergeant was like, and how aristocrats used to curse.

Cuttings and other notes

A commonplace book is for cuttings, images, photographs, cartoons or anything else that might be relevant to your writing project. A typical example is the experience of the writer's memory playing tricks. A story set in the 1950s might refer to children's sweets or comics; the writer needs to know these in visual terms. So cuttings from advertising are useful.

A case study on this is a project for a collection of poems written by Angie Milton. She wanted to write a series of lyrics and meditative poems on the idea of disfigurement or ugliness, in contrast to the dominant images of perfect bodies and ideal beauty put forward by the mass media. She went through three stages of work:

1. Gathering: a commonplace book was filled with random images from magazines, and medical photographs of bruises, wounds, or facial disfigurement.
2. A small anthology of lines and images from writings on the subject was collected.
3. The notebook was used for drafts of prose that would eventually emerge into poems.

This is not to make it all sound easy. I want to stress the need for organisation and method as well as disciplined application to writing.

Time and effort

What has become obvious here is that creative writing is tough work. Few people realise just how much energy and stamina is enquired. Many writers work for considerable time in longhand on drafts, then still more time at the keyboard as the better drafts emerge.

> For this reason, a useful habit is to take regular short breaks from writing;

to walk around and unwind. Too much concentration over long periods becomes unproductive. But one thing is certain: the myth of inspiration has to be dispelled here. The question is, do we wait for the Muse to call, or do we invite her in? You can see from these points about drafts and observation that the usual view is that waiting for her to call is usually a formula for failure.

Your one-volume reference

The commonplace book may be arranged in a variety of ways, but go through this thinking first:

1. Ask yourself what you actually *know*. *Good writing is about something*. Readers tire of vagueness and abstraction, however high the imagination soars. Write a list of what you know well – it might be how to lay concrete or what the capitals of the major states are. It might be how to change a nappy or pour a pint of beer from a pump. Whatever knowledge you have will help in producing authentic writing.

2. List technical terms from one of these subjects. Log just how much specific vocabulary there is to be used in writing. Everything has a name and these words add power and feeling (and a sense of reality) for the reader. For instance, the metal end of a shoe-lace is an aglet. Seamus Heaney uses dialect words sometimes, like *pampooties* (shoes) to give the feel of place and regional awareness.

3. Rate your subjects according to their potential as subjects for interesting writing topics. (Note your reasons for making these decisions also).

Keeping a personal anthology

Finally, here is one more suggestion for gathering a personal library of writing resources BBC Radio 4 has an occasional series called *With Great Pleasure*. In this, a celebrity chooses favourite pieces of writing for a personal anthology. This is a very useful idea for a writer at any stage in their career. Why is this? Mainly because your responses to words signpost your writing skills.

Organise your anthology of quotes, texts and extracts around your habitual preoccupations. What topics always interest you? In my case, my anthology has these headings:

Arrival/strangers/families/Yorkshire/Jewish humour/travel by sea/Spain

These tend to be things I come back to again and again when exploring writing ideas. Find your own preoccupations. Note which parts of a daily newspaper you always o to first; which shelves in the library do you always walk to? What conversation topics interest you and why? What type of photographs absorbs you most? All these are pointers to what might make up a commonplace book. For some, these provide images which settle deeply in the individual imagination. Therefore the writer returns many times to these images, finding more interest there on every visit.

Songs may also play a part in this. Fiction writers often say that a narrative in a song triggered an idea for a story or even a novel. But in many cases, it is the interest in a strong image that is preserved. Obviously, the real advantage of this is that you can open the page with the image in front of you when you eventually sit down to write.

Tutorial

Progress questions
1. How would you describe your writing voice? Find some adjectives to describe it.
2. Why is looking at subjects with 'new' perspectives so useful to writers?

Discussion points
1. Is parody an acceptable genre of writing in itself?
2. What do you see as the purpose of 'imitation'?

Practical assignments

1. Find a writer's notebook in print. Then compare rough note with a finished work. What do you learn from seeing tha process?

2. Investigate writing that writers have disowned or wante scrapped (Auden's poetry is full of examples). What is to b learned from this idea of the impossibility of writing the fu reality of a thing?

3. Look at ways in which writers reflect on their art i notebooks. Are these always enlightening or are there danger in writing too much reflection?

Study tip

1. As you read notebooks in print, note how much writing i concerned with different perceptions (visual, auditory, olfactory intellectual etc.).

2. compare the 'literary' with the natural and functional. The classi example is Wordsworth's poem 'Daffodils'. Compare the poen with his sister Dorothy's journal entry on the same subjec (*Journals of Dorothy Wordsworth* – Thursday, 15 April, 1802.). The were both together at Gowbarrow in Cumbria. William's writin; was consciously literary, Dorothy's was merely descriptive. Wha is to be learned about the authentic sense in writing from this?

****

3

Practice in Prose

One-minute summary – Regardless of what you want to write in prose, from autobiography to fiction, the basis will be the skills that all effective writing relies on. This means paying attention to the elements of all creative language. The first step is to ask what characterises *creative* language. We then look at ways of honing skills and developing confidence in generating interest, difference and potency at the level of the sentence and paragraph, before building up to complete prose works. Most writers need these initial stages, even though the aim might be to write poetry. Description and evocation are always needed. The focus o the chapter is to look at ways of creating life and interest in words, even when they deal with familiar things or perfunctory actions.

In this chapter you will learn:

➤ How to develop a personal 'voice'.

➤ How to make interest and freshness in describing subjects.

Short pieces of reflection
Transmuting the familiar

One of the trickiest issues in creative writing is the point about what characterises it. How does it express the qualities we think of when we say the phrase? The base notions and to make a distinction between functional vocabulary and creative. Words and sentences used in a vehicle repair manual obviously need to be clear and precise, as do legal phrases. The necessity to say 'In the following document, the legal entity referred to is taken to be the estate of John Smith' precludes the *embellishment* of the meaning. So 'creative' implies a sense of ornamentation, of adding additional perspectives to the functional statement itself. These comparisons make the point:

1. Functional statement:
   The football is made of leather.
2. Additional perspective:
   The football is made of strong, durable leather.
   (two adjectives have been added, but both only provide simple informative meanings).
3. The adored football is made of strong, durable leather:
   Now, one emotive adjective adds a creative dimension because it has two elements:

   (a) Individuation and (b) an implication of the football leading to other interests.

This is very basic, but it highlights the tendency for creative language to be imaginative, emotive and open-ended. Try this with any famous line of poetry and the features are easily seen: 'Shall I compare thee to a summer's day'? But prose does not always make these qualities so evident. Here is an example of how effective and creative prose enhances the familiar by adding these things:

Houses have moods: this one, where I was born, had rages and sulks.

As with so much creative writing, the heart of this is an image. The house is seen as a living organism in some way. Undoubtedly, the source of the creative dimension in this writing is often metaphysical something moving away from literal meaning. Creative writing always has a tendency to shift from direct reference and literal statement:

Literal: he was a very aged man.

Metaphorical: he was as old as the hills.

But we need to go further. All the discussion of notebooks and research in the previous chapter was to clear the ground for the fundamental aim of writing: to define the 'thingness', the essential inner life of something. The reader wants to share perceptions and also to be helped to look again, or to look towards something they may never meet in their actual experience. This is why, for instance Stephen King defines storytelling quite simply as 'telepathy'.

Reflect and re-express

With these points in mind, now try some short paragraphs of reflection on familiar everyday events. You might take the example of a visit to a friend or a walk through town. Try to think of a first short statement as the opening of the 'voice' you are aiming at:

Barwell town centre is a fallen world. Everything gradually sinks towards ruin and decay. Even attempts at renewal have failed, as the place loses its sense of itself with every new piece of red brick. What was a northern town ten years ago is now like a corner of a Mid-West town in the States.

Notice how the first short sentence hints at the treatment of the subject as the paragraph gathers a driving pulse of attitude. This comes from being clear about two basic things before writing prose:

Is my attitude clear to me?

Do I want to reveal something as I write or reinforce what I already think?

As a general rule, the best creative writing comes from the reader having a sense that he or she is thinking, feeling, groping towards a truth and a feeling as the text advances. This is the opposite of that sense of a writer being totally sure of everything and delivering a set of finished, well-entrenched notions.

Making the ordinary strange

A literary school of theory, the Russian Formalists, considered this aim to make the essential existence of a thing the heart of imaginative writing. How do you make the stoniness of the stone apparent? Again, there are degrees of exactitude:

1. The stone was grey.
2. The stone was full of quartz clusters.
3. The stone reminded me of my friend's heart.

But the question remains, how do we make the familiar interesting? The answer is tough but not impossible. Writers have a massive array of resources to help in this struggle for truth and exactitude. Here is one suggestion that can be the basis of some practice writing in your notebook:

31

Task: To write about a character in both general and specific ways.
Example:
<u>General</u>
Tom Swift was a product of his time. Thatcher's Britain made him yearn for expensive suits, a huge salary and an ego the size of one of the shabby new tower blocks emerging in the city.
<u>Specific</u>
Tom Swift was a tall man, pock-marked from teenage acne. His face was always red, as if he was constantly coming in from the bright sun.

This basic technique can be practised with any subject you like: what you aiming at is making grand statements and also precise ones running through a range of verbal skills as you practise. Look at the openings of your favourite prose works and see how characters are depicted or explained.

The art of description
In the eighteenth century, a prose writer had rules about writing. For most, it was a matter of reflecting and producing the elegancies of classical writers' styles. Therefore, if one wanted to be rhetorical there was Cicero as a model; if the aim was politics, there was Seneca or Caesar, and so on. But the English language is always in flux, and the innovators come along. Daniel Defoe came along and wrote a workmanlike, authentic style made for a more everyday world of commerce and conversation, and so, although it is hard for us to see it now, the opening of *Robinson Crusoe* (1719) is highly original and most innovative in its time.

'I was born in the year 1632, in the City of York, of a good family, though not of that country, my father being a foreigner of Bremen, who settled first at Hull'.

This is factual, direct and functional, but of course, it is an imagined voice from a world the readers would see as part of their world. It is familiar yet somehow indicative of an entrancing story yet to come.

Bringing alive

Usually, simplicity does the trick. Most of us describe what is there. If we do that well enough, the result will be successful and effective writing. But should we always stand on tiptoe to make something especially interesting? Not as a rule: the better plan is to make simplicity create interest. The art of description has always been concerned with this.

The most commonly used techniques are those that evoke the senses. We try to give the reader the smell, taste, colour, dimensions of something. But there are other methods. These are the most common, and it pays to practise them all – on your own selected topics of course:

1. Sense

   Example: Going into that flat was like a visit to a run-down pet shop. There was a sense of mammal-stink, though I could see only children, stomping around in soiled nappies. One was eating some kind of custard from the floor.

2. Metaphor

   Example: The whole room was like a space capsule. Every surface was clinical, metallic. There was more chrome than in a dentist's surgery. Tall white cabinets filled the space; there was no human clutter on the work-tops. It was a cabin ready for take-off, well away from humanity.

3. Abstraction

   Example: The hall was packed with people listening to every word from the suited man at the lectern. I thought of light and eternal, endless space. A great emptiness filled me and the place, as boredom brought on yawns as big as eternity. Great hours stretched away like the Milky Way as the words came across like clouds of morphine.

There are many ways to describe something, and it is a skill never to be under-rated. Work away at it, sentence by sentence. Some of the oldest rules of writing help in this, such as the notions of only having one subject in each paragraph and having a topic or key sentence i each paragraph that is developed within that paragraph only:

The point I reached on the mountain was now a little nerve-racking. knew that I must not look down. The cars way below would be like insects knew that my head would want to spin. The wind made things worse: I felt unsteady that the slightest puff of air would make my heart pound wi apprehension.

Defamiliarise

Another interesting stylistic exercise is to write about something fror a strange or odd perspective. For instance, imagine someone is abou to take a penalty at a Sunday football match. These things are goin on around that area as he prepares to take the kick:

A train is passing and someone looks out of the window.
A sea-gull flies overhead.
A child is flying a kite nearby.
A man clears up litter, thinking personal thoughts, unconcerned.
The manager of the team prays for the ball to go in the net.

And so on…

Think how writing from one of these other perspectives adds interes The opening of Ian MacEwen's novel, *Enduring Love,* begins with range of varying perspectives on the same event.

From concept to written word

Let us return to the point made earlier, that there is always a sense o never attaining what was aimed at in writing. Think how powerfull this applies to the art of description. Sometimes an insight is sho but authentic:

His imagination was like a hawk, watching for something to drop on and devour.
Or, a sentence can build with layers, moving closer to completeness:
The car was coated in rust; the doors were flaking at the corners; little fragments orange flakes flicked off every time the door was opened; the bonnet was like piece of fabric. Fraying at the edges with ruddy tatters.

The best advice is to work on paragraphs in the notebook; take an observation that started with a mere glance of interest, then develop this into a paragraph with a strong presence and a sense of authenticity.

Tutorial
Progress questions
1. What factors make up a sense of a writing voice?
2. What methods are available for enhancing descriptive writing?

Points for discussion
1. What do you consider to be the real interest in the language we call 'creative'?
2. Does interesting imaginative writing always have to surprise or shock? Or can it merely reinforce what we could or should think?
3. Think again about what Defoe achieved. Compare this with a writer who tries to startle or bully the reader into seeing the character as bizarre or weird. What are the dangers of trying too hard to be interesting or to be notably different? Look at some highly original works such as James Joyce's *Finnegan's Wake* or Emyr Humphrie's *A Toy* Epic to see some of this style.

Practical assignments
1. Read some of the best acknowledged describers in writing, such as Laurie Lee in *Cider with Rosie*, or any of Thomas Hardy's openings to novels. List the techniques used.
2. Find openings to prose works that use (a) huge panoramic perspectives and (b) close, 'tight' description, intense to the subject. Consider the effects and responses these create.

Study tips
1. In your personal anthology collection, find and preserve the most effective descriptions you find in the category or genre that you most want to write.
2. Think about innovative writing – the kind that tries to describe only by inference, never saying directly what the topic is. You

could try this in your notebook; see if you can write fou
sentences without being clear about the topic. You might preten
to be a visitor from mars looking for the first time at a familia
object. (See Craig Raine' poem *A Martian Sends a Postcard Home* fo
an example).

****

4

Practice in Poetry

One-minute summary – If you want to write poetry of any kind, there are profound rewards in doing so: poetry is a matter of structured emotion, dealing with minimal statements of complex chains of thought. The rewards and satisfactions are often related to the human love of form and rhythm. For this reason, the material covered in this chapter is intended to introduce both formal and 'free' verse. There is also an explanation of the necessary habits and mind-set required for writing poetry. This is a kind of receptivity, and openness to random, experimental thinking. Finally, I suggest working on a three-stage structure in the early phase of writing poetry. Of course, all this writing depends on the individual's reasons for writing poetry; usually these are not related to career plans, but there are writers who have made a hole writing life from poetry, so the art is not necessarily a simple one meant for a 'hobby'.

In this chapter, you will learn:

➢ How to develop poetic subjects.

➢ How to work from drafts to lines.

➢ The characteristics of formal verse.

➢ How to work with metrics and syllabics.

Free verse
The concept
Looking at the layout of free verse on a page, it is easy to believe that poetry like this is chaotic. Many students have suggested that free verse is simply 'chopped-up prose'. Bad free verse may be so, but the real thing has several features that make it a natural form for expressing feeling. To explain what it is, there is a need to start with the idea of form itself.

In poetry composition through the centuries, English writer were given a classical education and this meant the study of the Gree and Roman authors. These poets worked according to rules about th rhythm in lines of verse. Later in the chapter, we look at this syster of 'metrics' but for now, the point is that free verse is not constraine by these rules.

Rules but no rules

Rather than being governed by metrics, as in this **stanza**:

> *I sit beneath your leaves, old oak;*
> *You mighty one of all the trees,*
> *Beneath whose hollow trunk,*
> *A man could stable his big horse with ease.*
> (W H Davies: *The Oak Tree*)

Free verse is a way of writing that follows inner modulations of voic rather than a set pulse of beats. Notice how the Davies poem ha four syllables in each line, and when you read it aloud, it has 'regular' (repeated) beat. It is in a stanza, a section of a poem, set ou usually with regularity.

Free verse follows the pulse of inner talk, or of speech Effects are often like this:

> *That was the way the world went,*
> *Then,*
> *When smiles were free*
> *And you felt them true.*

Notice how in these lines, the words are expressed and lineated according to the nature of the statements.

So how 'free' is free verse?

It can be seen from this that free verse does have an organising principle. There are some guidelines. People who are critical of free verse defend formal structures by saying that form 'stops a poem saying everything'. Yet advocates of free verse claim there is just as much discipline and hard work behind their lyrics. There are features that define good quality free verse:

> ➤ A sense of authentic intonation.
> ➤ The use of significant pauses to follow the emotion behind the words.
> ➤ Use of 'white space' to direct the reader.
> ➤ A direct, often confessional feel, the poet speaking honestly.

An ideal poetics for beginners

Every poet has his or her own *poetics*: a personal credo about how they perceive poetry and what the composition of the art is for them. Poetics is a compound of personal imagination, prior formative reading and philosophic reflection. Once again, this is where the notebook becomes valuable. This is because free verse is ideal as a first step: a poet can start with prose drafts, then extract the lines from that, for instance:

Prose draft:
The feeling of being at home yet somehow a stranger in this city. Faces vaguely familiar – they should be my people but I don't have a sense of belonging anymore, like my father...

First free verse draft:

A second of comfort,
Then a shiver of strangeness.
A citizen and a stranger;
My father's belonging
Like a well-loved jacket.
But I can't find clothes to fit here.

The free verse draft has extracted the basic feeling, then used the metaphor of clothes, as something suggesting comfort and ease. It still needs more work. But free verse like this is ideal for the first step in poetry writing, as it allows you to be direct, yet play with metaphorical vocabulary. It's a start that has fun element., a playfulness.

Some short forms

In contrast, what about the first step in formal poetry? There are tw
basic principles. These are:

1. Syllabic poems
   Here the idea is simply to count the syllables per line:
   Summer has red gowns,
   Wears the starry bracelets well.
   Who thinks of the dead?

This is a haiku, a short form originally from Japan, having three line
with a syllable pattern of 5/7/5. Count the syllables of the three line
and you will have that count. Notice that there is no repeated beat o
a rhythm, and there is no rhyme at the ends of the lines.

Poet can invent a syllabics form quite easily; simply think of
stanza count and line count; so you might have a poem constructe
with this patter:

Stanza 1 - 668866   Stanza 2 – 664466   Stanza 3 – 668866

The permutations are almost infinite. But the art of this is in
matching the syllable count with the subject and the emotive drive o
the poem.

There are several short syllabic forms to use when you star
writing. These are the commonest:

The haiku and the tanka

As just explained, this is a three-lined poem, originally a meditationa
lyric, reflecting on nature or general observation of life. A useful wa
to work is to practice by writing in response to a photograph o
painting. Use this approach:

1. Choose a photograph in the social documentary category; a
   subject such as civil disorder, war, conflict, or even poverty.
2. Study the image and imagine that you are someone actuall
   arriving at the scene and witnessing the event.
3. Write down your responses in prose.
4. Try to extract the three dominant responses for working on a
   haiku.

A tanka is simply a haiku with two extra lines, each of seven syllables, so we have a pattern of 5/7/5/7/7:

Too many times this,
The sad faces of children;
Lives undone by war,
Like a frown on their small dreams;
Like a cloud across their lawn.

The englyn

This is a Welsh form, and with this we have the freedom of a total syllable count, so the challenge is to write four lines, totalling 30 syllables.

Leaving home again, and snow on the ground;
I said my goodbyes too many times, too loudly.
But this time, silent – it's my last.

Notice how, if the middle line is slightly longer, the final line is short, and therefore carries the emotional 'clinch' thought more effectively.

The cinquain

Originally a French form, this is another popular syllabic poem for poets trying out their skills. The line pattern is 2/4/6/8/2, so you can see at a glance what the idea is: very long line as a penultimate, then a two-syllable closure:

Today,
A day to love,
Our own time together.
Nothing can take the sun away:
It's you.

Tripartite structures

It is very helpful when learning the art of poetry in this way to work in terms of three stages of thought or feeling. This is very basic, following the beginning/middle/end of a simple story, but there is rather more to it than that. I suggest:

Stage one: *establish interest through oppositions.*
Stage two: *complicate and invite reader-involvement.*
State three: *resolve and clarify* or *resolve and open up thought.*

This can be best shown in a free verse poem:

Waiting Room
Here, they all gather to share some dead time.
Staring vacantly at mortal reminders,
Texts in urgent red or glossy black.
The nestling child tugging at mum's arm;
Sad teenager nursing a loving wound;
The hacking, over-coated old-timer,
All here between attempts at living.
And me? Hat about the scribbling writer?
I see all our ropes being twisted tighter.

The first three lines establish a scene; the next four lines add a sense of urgent life and a problematic human centre to the room then the last couplet adds a statement about the nature of observing and indeed, of writing itself.

Writing in metre

Now we come to the notion of metrical verse, as in the W H Davies piece earlier in the chapter. In English poetry, there are four commonly-used *metrical feet;* these are the basis of a great deal of classic English poetry, and the reference is to the clusters of syllables which are repeated in a metrical line. Each metrical foot has a pattern of stressed and unstressed syllables. For instance:

Iambic – unstressed/stressed shown as: - /   as in the word **unknown**

Trochaic - stressed/unstressed shown as   / -   as in the word **never**

Dactylic - stressed/unstressed/unstressed shown as: /- -   as in the word **sweltering**

42

Anapaestic - unstressed/unstressed/stressed shown as: - - /   as in the word **unresolved**

There is no regulation insisting that all poets know and use these, but poems using these metres are always worth trying, as an intellectual exercise, to try out your skill. All I want to do here is take one example of how and why metrical poetry is of interest: the form of the sonnet.

Look up more information on this and other forms in Richard Cochrane's *Studying Poetry* in the Studymates series if you want to know more. For the present purposes, I am including this one example, and this is the Shakespearean sonnet, with a pattern of 14 lines having a *rhyme-scheme* (a pattern of words ending each line and rhyming in certain ways). This is a perfect example of a tripartite structure, and using metrical skill:

Shall I compare thee to a summer's day?
Thou art more lovely and more temperate.
Rough winds do shake the darling buds of May
And summer's lease hath all to short a date.
Sometime too hot the eye of heaven shines,
And often is his gold complexion dimmed;
And every fair from fair sometime declines,
By chance, or nature's changing course untrimmed;
But thy eternal summer shall not fade,
Nor lose possession of that fair thou ow'st,
Nor shall Death brag though wanderest in his shade,
When in eternal lines to time thou grow'st.
So long as men can breathe and eyes can see,
So long lives this, and this gives life to thee.

The rhyme scheme is **ABABDCCDEFEFGG,** the letters indicating the rhymes and how they work. The convention is to call the first end-rhyme A and through as far as the poem goes.

The metre is in iambic pentameter; that is that the metrical feet are mostly iambic, and the lines have five feet each. The commonest line-lengths are:

Dimeter	-	two feet
Trimeter	-	three feet
Tetrameter	-	four feet
Pentameter	-	five feet
Hexameter	-	six feet

In a sonnet we can see the tripartite structure perfectly:

Stage one	-	*establish the beauty of the person addressed*
Stage two	-	*introduce the idea of change and decay in all nature*
Stage three	-	*assert the power of art to create a kind of immortality c*
the subject		

East and west: having and being

What we have not done yet is discuss the basis of poetic writing. B this I mean the necessity for a poet to understand the nature of poetic text, regardless of form or convention. Every writer has personal viewpoint on this; personally, I feel it helps to consider th fundamental thinking and feeling processes in expressing the natur of *being* rather than *having*. In Erich Fromm's seminal book, *To Have* to Be? (see bibliography), he stresses the negative effects on creativit brought about by the materialism of the west. Looking to the easter forms like the haiku and tanka, he relates this writing to the centralit of being.

In other words, the human basis of poetry composition deeply embedded in the self and self-understanding. Most poetr comes from the urge to express feelings beyond normal verb; expression. Therefore, to cultivate the habit of writing poetry need all the disciplines and habits discussed in my opening chapter.

The most successful poems will therefore emerge from th testing out of emotions and responses to life – testing fore th authenticity of the thought or emotion. Nothing is so transparent i creative writing as the poem written from rhetoric rather than tru feeling. Having said that, there are definitely levels of subjects an styles in poetry: you might decide that you are one of these fc instance:

The private poet: Intensely concerned with the subjects deep in the self; mainly an autobiographical, reflective writer. Sylvia Plath would be an example.

The public poet: Concerned with the world of power and politics; with he arena where ideas and ideologies meet. Kipling would be an example.

Tutorial

Progress questions
1. What are the distinguishing features of free verse?
2. What are the three major metrical feet in English poetry?
3. Why would dimeter be only rarely used in a poem?

Points for discussion
Why is it almost always pointless to write a poem absolutely strictly according to metrical forms?

Practical assignments
1. Free verse has the virtue of being written in such a way that it can only be read in one way: the poet directs the reading closely. Find some classic free verse, such as work by Walt Whitman or D H Lawrence, and test this out by reading aloud.
2. Read more widely in the sonnet form and note the differences in rhyme-scheme, but also note the difference between those that use a final rhyming couplet and those that end with a quatrain (four line stanza or section).

Study tips
1. Read and consider some of the varieties of poetry and of poets. Be aware of the whole spectrum, and what the range of publication outlets tends to be. Useful places to look for this are the magazines, such as *Poetry Review* and *P N Review* (see

bibliography). But also look for poetry on CD, in its guise a
performance poetry.

2. When you find a poem you admire, work on your own poem i
   the 'template' manner discussed earlier, and then read aloud. A
   you read, you will detect any weak diction or imagery, and you wi
   also learn about the intonations of free verse more easily with thi
   type of practice.

****

5

Gathering the Right Resources

One-minute summary: Now we turn to the range of publications, organisations and educational sources that are there to help you establish yourself and your writing. This is a massive diversity of support groups and businesses ready to help you, and writers just starting out need considerable guidance around this ever-expanding area of publishing and appraisal work. We look now at what other professionals can offer you in terms of helping you to find critical feedback, readership and publication. But we also look at a range of steps you can take, and just how much self-help may achieve if you know what you want to write, for whom, and in what forms or media.

In this chapter you will learn:

➤ What is available in print and on the internet to help you.

➤ What should determine your use and selection of these sources.

➤ How you can obtain useful feedback or tuition in writing.

➤ How you can save time and money by planning sensibly.

Reference works and magazines
All is confusion: a culture of choice

Most aspiring writers very sensibly go to books for help in the first instance; it is logical for writers to look for words of advice: the written word in handbooks and the spoken word in the increasingly common 'writer's workshop' or even in such places as radio talks and internet sites. But the most convenient place to start is on the bookshelves in the library or the local bookshop. There you will find a plethora of 'how to' books much like this one. But very few of them spend much time on the first difficulty you will encounter: how to choose what to write. Aspirin writers arguably fall into three categories:

1. The person who 'wants to write' but has no idea what to write.
2. The person who likes telling stories, reads in certain genres, and to write the same.
3. The person who knows that there is a 'book in them' and enjoys research, planning and talking about writing, but doesn't settle on anything specific.

Quite frankly, there is a great deal of talking and thinking about writing, and not so much in print that actually signals to the reader that 'this book will help you choose'. So before you start reading anything in addition to this book – that is, something more specific than this general guide – consider this imaginary case study.

Joe Bloggs: wannabe writer

Phase one: Joe has been reading a lot lately about people who have got themselves big book deals with their 'first novel'. Well, teachers and friends always said that he could write. Why not find out more? After all, Joe reads fiction every week, loves a gripping thriller or a murder story, and they don't seem that difficult to write, surely?

Phase two: Find out more. He starts in the local library and the internet. The library has two shelves of books on 'How to Write a Novel' themes, or 'Discover the Writer Within' approach He looks at some but can't recognise his situation in there. The internet throws up thousands of sites dedicated to writing and writers. There are also correspondence courses advertised. Then, on a desk in the library he sees various leaflets about courses in creative writing being offered at the local college or university.

Phase three: Joe has gathered all these things and on his desk he now has pile of leaflets, a stack of sheet downloaded from the internet and several handbooks.

Result: Confusion.

What Joe should have done is sat down with a notepad and listed exactly what some of his aims might be. For instance, fundamentals questions about aims are priceless.

You might ask yourself:

What do I genuinely want to write? What kind of thing?
What do I know already about this writing – as a reader?
Who teaches and/or publishes exactly that kind of writing?

If you write your own answers to these questions the result will be a profile of you and your aims. For instance, suppose someone decided they could write a whodunit. Specifically, a whodunit without too much police procedure, as they have no knowledge of that. But the story would be set in Oxford because the writer knows the city well. A walk around a bookshop would tell them who publishes exactly that version of whodunit. The book they want now is 'How to Write Crime Fiction', with the whodunit chapter in focus. The web sites needed are ones dedicated to that particularly writing.

Categories of material in print

Now you are setting up your stall as a writer. You have focused more. Maybe your range is not one specific thing; you might have decided on writing short stories and aiming at the small magazines, with a view to eventually writing the firs novel, when you learn by writing stories. You may have decided that feature articles are your specialism, but you now need some pinpointed subjects. Whatever your decision, you need some essential reading and reference. These are the standard recommendations:

Reference:

You need a good dictionary. This means one that has full information about words in it: not a simple definition. You need a book that gives usage examples and the full range of different meanings. A thesaurus is invaluable also. Here you have useful groupings of words with similar meanings (synonyms).

You need a writing reference book with all the professional information in one place, and you have two to choose from, both published annually:

Barry Turner, *The Writer's Handbook* (Macmillan) and/or *The Writers' and Artists' Yearbook* (A & C Black).

Barry Turner's book has more information on a wider range of topics than the other; but essentially, either book would provide the contact details and descriptions of all major publishers, independent publishers, agents and supporting services, together with legal information on copyright, contracts and so on.

Finally, how useful are the writing magazines? There are several of these, two always available in the high street, and some by subscription. A typical issue will cover most aspects of writing, editing and publishing, and have hundreds of advertisements for courses, writing groups and small press publications. In a typical issue. you might find only one or two articles that match your writing interests. So look around and decide for yourself, but the value of these magazines cannot be under-estimated, for these reasons, they give you:

➤ Up-dated information on markets
➤ Contact details of professionals
➤ Advice on specific writing genres and categories by professional writers or editors
➤ Competitions and details of prizes
➤ Information about professional societies

The main magazines are included in my bibliography.

Critical feedback

All writers, at all stages of their career, need some sense of a response to what they do. But in the first stages of writing, an appraisal is essential. It is too easy to have the tactful approval of friends, and to be told that something was 'really good' tells you nothing at all except that what you wrote pleased one person. There are several sources of feedback, all offering different kinds of appraisal.

Critiquing circles: Here members circulate one typescript at a time, so every member has their turn. Supposing that you have completed your story, novel, poems etc. You circulate the text, and comments from others will normally be anonymous. This arrangement often happens as a spin-off from a writers' group, but you will also see postal groups or internet groups trying the same exercise.

This mechanism has a huge advantage over any face-to-face feedback at a course or workshop, in that the anonymity enhances a true sense of impartial comment, of course. Even at a workshop, that can be difficult to obtain.

Writing workshops: These may be one-off events, or sometimes part of a short course in which workshops are integrated. These can take various forms, but basically all contributors write something at or for the session, then perhaps read an extract aloud, and others take notes. Then a general discussion takes place, at which the writer in focus takes copious notes regarding drafting, editing, style and other matters.

Correspondence course: typical example of this is the Open College of Arts, who offer a course called *Starting to Write.* In this, students have detailed feedback on assignments set. If you want to be a student doing a structured course, rather than simply writing what you want and finding feedback, this is for you. There are many others, and I have listed the main ones in the reference section.

Honesty the best policy

Most response and feedback goes on informally, of course. Maybe a group of friends attend the local classes run by the WEA or college. They are working on their own writing projects, and they read each others' work. Naturally, there will be feedback, and a tutor will try to instil the good practice of being honest, and therefore being thick-skinned when it comes to your own work being considered. But the point is a simple one: writers want to learn from the experience, and to be able to feel free to discuss ideas and technique honestly and openly. There are some useful guidelines for any such gathering or appraisal situation:

➢ Be honest but objective
➢ Keep to language and style, not biographical factors
➢ Avoid any personal writing in group interaction
➢ Find individual feedback from a third party as well as from the regular group
➢ Be open-minded and prepared to learn

Many students of creative writing, at least in my experience of over twenty years of teaching the subject, feel not only unable to read their work aloud, but also claim that reading other work adversely influences their own style. Stephen King has reservations about such feedback, but it's useful to bear in mind the advice given by the poet and playwright, Adrian Mitchell, to new writers: he said that they should read a lot, write a little, read a lot more, write a little, and keep on until it gets better.

Writing Courses

Varieties

There is plenty of choice here. These are the main types on offer:

1. *Courses in educational institutions*

Creative writing courses are now offered almost everywhere by these groups:

The university
The college of further education
The Workers' Educational Association
Adult Education
Distance learning from universities and private businesses

These types of courses will tend to have certification of some kind; that is, you may gain Credit Accumulation Transfer points which could be in whole or part of a standard qualification. Therefore, sometimes there is an academic requirement in the course. This often means an element of *commentary* and the submission of rough drafts for assessment.

Obviously, you need to look into these things when deciding whether or not a specific course would help you. A marked contrast is seen, for instance, between a typical WE course a certified university course, though both cater for beginners. The course in adult education will be quite relaxed, with a stress placed on discussion of work, set assignments and individual help. It may have a more leisurely and a more clearly-defined role for the tutor, as well as very specific course objectives.

2. *Leisure/short courses*

A typical April edition of *Writers' Forum* magazine has dozens of residential courses advertised. These may take place in the private sector, on a campus, or as part of an annual programme run by a writers' group. They have certain special features which prove attractive to new writers, as they tend to offer:

More time spent with the tutor
More opportunity for socialising and informal talk

Opportunities for making contact with many professionals in creative writing

Short but intensive tuition in a designated topic

For instance, the programme for 2003 at Caerleon Writers' Holiday (one week) included five-session courses on Starting to Write, Breaking into Travel Writing, Making Money from Writing, Writing Poetry, Writing Scripts for TV and Writing Biography. Other places might offer a complete weekend of talk and tuition focused on one genre or skill. Many of these take place in July and August but there are courses operating at any time of the year if you search the course listings on the internet.

Societies

Brief mention should be made of those societies who take an interest in either one genre or one author. *The Writers' Handbook* lists around a hundred of these groups, and as part of their work, many provide special seminars and talks about the skills involved. A typical example would be the British Society of Comedy Writers, who hold conferences regularly, and involve agents, editors and publishers. The Romantic Novelists' Association has a similar programme. It is worth being a member of such a group once you are sure of your speciality and have already tried some writing and had feedback.

Writing Circles
What does a writers' group do?

A simple way to answer this question is to note that the National Association of Writers' Groups (a registered charity) notes that its activities involve competitions, producing a newsletter, produces anthologies and holds a large-scale festival of writing annually. In other words, a typical writers' group or circles is all about communication, networking and professional advancement. Even on the smallest scale, such as a meeting of three people in a small village to read and discuss their writing, there is learning, communication and sharing of knowledge and ideas in progress.

Benefits?

Any conference obviously has the benefits of communication and learning about such things as what editors are looking for or which publisher is starting a list in which genre. But regular attendance at a circle meeting and receiving a newsletter has several benefits:

➤ Up-dates on marketing and submissions
➤ News of new publications
➤ Booking details for courses and conferences
➤ Competition information
➤ Links with writers with similar interests to you

~The last point cannot be overestimated; writing is a lonely business most of the time, and most writers tend to gravitate towards one or two categories or markets; consequently, a chance to meet and share ideas with someone who writes exactly the same material is worth having. Circles, groups and societies all provide this.

Thinking in advance

Another point worth making is that when you start submitting work for publication, at any level, you will find that there is a certain amount of having to think in terms of the future. For instance, a vogue in medieval historical fiction, with books on the shelves today, may have gone next year, and no publisher wants to know about your manuscript. In 2002, editors and publishers were mostly talking about whether the 'Chicklit' boom following Helen Fielding's *Bridget Jones's Diary* was receding or not. One fiction editor, talking at a writers' conference in that year, guessed that something called 'Henlit' was now coming. A lot of heads bent down and things were scribbled in dozens of writers' notebooks on that occasion.

Of course, all this is guesswork, even by editors> But as a writer, you will be writing what comes naturally to you – or will you? Many people start out with that approach. You write what you want to write and then find the market. But increasingly, his is being reversed. Most handbooks advise writing three chapters and a synopsis of your book, and then finding a publisher or an agent is the next step.

Tutorial
Progress questions
1. What are the main considerations when gathering and using reference works?
2. How can feedback be made more objective?

Points for discussion
What factors come into play when deciding on taking a writing course? What aims should come first?

Practical assignments
1. Survey the writing courses offered by universities. How do they describe their activities? List the professional elements offered in relation to those covering writing skills (eg publishing industry, legal information and so on).
2. Write to an arts association or organisation and ask for a newsletter and information about activities. Find out what tuition is built into activities.

Study tips
1. Go to a one-off talk on writing arranged in your area. Take notes on skills, marketing and submission. Compare these with advice in handbooks published ten years ago, and note the differences.
2. Visit a writers' group and make notes on how they operate their appraisal sessions. Monitor how the session is managed, and what benefits individuals appear to derive from these activities.

6
Ready for Print?

One-minute summary: When the preparatory thinking and planning has been done, and decisions have been made about what you want to write and why, then a point comes when a writer begins submitting work to editors and publishers. This chapter looks at this process and the decision-making that lies behind it. Too many authors rush to find outlets for their work; often this is because their skill and expertise have not reached the right level of quality. We consider here the 'invisible' learning that takes place in a writing career: comments from editors and information about your own personal voice and style, often given to you in fragments and asides, never formally. Finally, we look at the markets within markets: the range of options open to you as you wok towards seeing your writing in print.

In this chapter, you will learn:

➤ How to work out where and when to submit work
➤ How to focus on the right outlets
➤ The procedure for approaching editors

When and how to submit work
Self-assessment

This phase is one of the most difficult things for a writer to do: to actually assess the worth of one's writing. Think of the different criteria one may apply in order to answer that question. The issue might be of comparing your own work to what you have seen imprint; or it might be guided by advice from your peers or from tutors. There may even have been an appraisal from a professional company, and this might be very favourable.

But the tough question persists: is my work good enough to submit for publication? In the end, there are only so many basic steps you can take:

Re-read the text meticulously

Look closely for 'mechanical error': grammar, spelling and syntax

List the virtues you see in it: what has the piece to offer and to whom?

It is always a reasonably accurate guide to assess what the writing has gone through to be the text it is now, at the time you are ready to submit it for consideration. That is, what has been the drafting process? The next chapter looks closely at this.

Reasons for writing to an editor

Think of the reasons why someone would want to submit work for scrutiny by a stranger – a person who knows a specific readership much better than you do; a person who knows what his readers want and what works for that specific publication. The reference books do give you some minimal guidance. One poetry magazine once announced that 'It would look at passionate poetry of all kinds, but please, no more poetry about granddads'.

The editor/publisher you target will have a rationale, and accepted work falls in line with that in most cases. So the first step is to match what you have to offer with what exists. Basic errors like these do happen:

➤ Writers submit works on natural history or politics to fashion magazines.

➤ Writers submit stories of 10,000 words to publications with 2,000 word limits on contributions.

➤ Writers do write very long letters, telling their whole life story, to overworked editors.

It makes sense , therefore, to research the market and to make sure you read the publication to which you submit, or read the catalogue and lists of publisher you approach.

How to submit work

There are far too many unsolicited submissions landing on desks every day. Some of the figures quoted are daunting for the new writer. For instance, the features editor of *The Guardian* receives an average of fifty unsolicited articles a day; many London publishers of mass market fiction say they average one hundred scripts a week. A few of them employ an editor with special responsibility for the 'slush pile' – the name given to the heap of unagented submissions. Often, a junior editor looks at these and passes on the few promising ones to a senior colleague.

With this in mind, you need to do everything possible to strengthen your case, and for your script to be read. That is, if you are submitting work without having found an agent. (The companion volume to this, *Keep on Writing Professionally*, deals with agents and publishers in more depth). Here is some advice from experience on how to maximise your chances of success, regardless of what you write and who reads it:

1. Present a clean typescript. It should be in good English, well checked.
2. The format should be as requested, or according to normal practice: a margin with space for notes; text not permanently fastened, and the text protected in a folder.
3. Include a statement that you 'first British serial rights' as owner of the copyright of that work.
4. Include a short but informative letter about your writing aspirations and achievements so far.
5. Include a stamped, a self-addressed envelope for the return of the script.

Many editors specify what they want and they use a range of communication channels to tell the world: they might have a piece in a newsletter, or in a call for contributions, but in most cases, all you have is a few lines in one of the two main reference books.

Your letter: an example

Here is an example of the kind of letter you might write to accompany your work:

Dear Editor,

Please note the enclosed short story which I would like to submit for consideration. Could this be suitable for use in your publication? I regularly read the magazine, and I feel that his is written in a style suitable for your readers and your format.

I am a freelance writer specialising in short fiction and in biographical articles and profiles. I have had three pieces published in small magazines. Recently, I completed a course in creative writing at my local college.

I would appreciate your response to this piece.
Yours sincerely….

This is brief, relevant, and has just a little detail about who this writer is and what they have done so far. The comment about reading the publication shows an awareness of the readership and the policy and selection preferences of the editor(s).

Dealing with editors

This brings us to the subject of the editor. The editor or potential publisher of your work is very busy. Unless you are well-known or have submitted through an agent, the response if the work is rejected is likely to be short and without any helpful comment. Rejection may not necessarily mean that the writing is poor. Your work may be unsuitable for that publication; fashion or taste may be against it, it could be wrong time of year. The publication may have used a similar piece or published a similar book just a month ago.

On the other hand, an editor might write a few sentences that will at least guide you towards some sharpening of style or treatment in the work. What often happens is that you send out your work to several places. A stream of brief rejections follows. All hope seems gone, but then a letter arrives with several paragraphs of advice. Most successful writers talk about the editor who really helped them, took some time to advise and suggest things. Literary history is full of example in which the writer-editor relationship developed almost to a collaboration; famous examples are D H Lawrence and Edward Garnett, and Scott Fitzgerald and Maxwell Perkins. Certainly Jack Kerouac had an editor who crusaded for Kerouac being accepted, and gave him hours of his time and expertise. That was Malcolm Cowley. But for most of us, a few paragraphs that might point us to success are valuable indeed. You will know this is happening when you receive a paragraph like this:

We do not normally publish articles on this subject, but you have given this so much vitality and interest, that I feel you should show it to Joe Bloggs at The Blogger magazine, as he welcomes this style and approach. Do mention that I gave you his contact details...'

With this, you have that first inkling that maybe you are doing something right after all.

Personality and words

A point should be made also of the tone of the approach. How much of yourself should you put into professional correspondence? In general, if a relationship develops between editor/publisher and writer in which there is intellectual discussion and business mixes with taste and so on, this can only strengthen the collaboration. But the warning here is that an aspiring writer can go to excess in one of these habits:

The toady: do not flatter and lard your letter with compliments and superlatives.

The entertainer: do not show off your wonderful personality by telling jokes or personal anecdotes.

The special pleader: do not advertise your desperation or vanity before an editor.

It is true that an editor feels that it is important that the author has a personality, but the best advice is for the contributor to keep everything brief and businesslike unless the editor hints at another perspective on literary matters. The authors of this book have had experience of many types of editors, including some who ring up contributors for a chat and eventually ask for something to be written in two days please.

Networks again

A new writer needs some confidence and self-belief – in large quantities. You will inevitably collect rejection slips. But the market research is the crucial factor. Think of every contact, even an editor who rejects your work but asks to see more, as a potential contact. This pattern does emerge quite often in the freelance writer's world once some establishment has taken place and a few pieces have found print:

Stage one: submissions and letters are sent out at random.

Stage two: a refining process begins to emerge: more choice and selection of outlets tends to happen.

Stage three: scraps of feedback emerge and you start to receive invitations to submit work. For instance, the editor is planning a special issue of a subject he knows you write on.

Stage four: you write that piece and it is noticed by an editor of an anthology.

Some success stories may boost your confidence here. We have had a contributor to a magazine we edited whose work was seen by a London publisher in the small press; he has since published three novels. A student at a provincial university appeared at a local reading and was offered bookings at a prestigious folk club to read performance poetry. As with all the arts and creative subjects, persistence is a definite virtue, and one of your main assets, but it needs to be directed at the right aims and conceived with a sense of reality.

Specialism and choices

This hints at a return to the advice about being sure of your range and subjects. At this early stage of submitting work, cultivate the habit of meticulous filing and grouping of cuttings and research material. Much of what you have to do to meet the demands of an editor and his lists or publications involves re-writing. There is no time for the luxury of not wanting your style to be tampered with. There have been cases in which fiction writers have reduced stories of 8,000 down to 2,500 because an editor offered to publish on that basis.

This thinking invites discussion of the perennial question about 'the integrity of the artist'. Mainly, this relates to the mythic status of the 'Great Writer' created largely by the media. Our culture perpetuates the illusion of the inspired writer, the Creator, in a garret and usually suffering. Stories are disseminated about how the Great Writer was not published because the world of commerce wanted to interfere with the wonderful writing, and all because of a market. Well, there is another side to this, perhaps best exemplified by the career of Charles Dickens. Not only did he write for serialisation, but he changed endings after a massive public clamour for the death of Little Nell, in *The Old Curiosity Shop*, to be revoked, as happens at times in modern soap opera.

For these reason, it is worth facing up to the vagaries of the market, and the very tightly defined formats and writing styles of particular companies. Reasons for rejection will reflect this. You might have replies like this:

Your work is fine and we enjoyed it greatly, but it is too Anglo-centred for the current market

OR

While we thought that you created a really thrilling plot, the inclusion of a Russian Communist as the central character makes it unsuitable for our readers.

This may be hard to believe if you have been imbued with the *South Bank Show* perception for writing. Maybe a better lesson

63

is to recall the words of Mickey Spillane, who said: 'There are writers and there are authors. The difference is, writers get paid'.

Categories of markets
Back to your readers

In the opening chapter, we discussed the need to think closely about for whom you want to write. This returns now, with genuine and profound importance, as you consider which level or context your work fits into. This can best be illustrated by taking a case study: the short story.

Suppose you write short stories and you are simply at the first stage, developing any passing idea that seems to have potential, working out the plot and characters, and then wondering who might consider it for publication. These would be the most prominent markets available in Britain and the USA:

1. *The popular magazines such as women's weeklies and monthlies.*
2. *The literary magazines in London, Edinburgh, Dublin and Cardiff.*
3. *Provincial small magazines.*
4. *American literary magazines.*
5. *Radio fiction (limited almost exclusively to the BBC).*
6. *Fiction publishers.*

If the story is not tailored to any of these markets, there are various obstacles in your way here. Category 1: these publications have very specific needs and lengths, subjects and narrative ploys. Category 2: these would not normally take genre fiction and have clear policies and preferences related to their immediate cultures and briefs. Category 3: these provide your best chance of publication, but mostly do not pay for contributions. Category 4: you are having to compete with thousands of Americans, all fresh from creative writing courses and programs across a vast network of universities and writing groups. Category 5: stories for radio are mostly commissioned and are submitted via agents or production companies. Finally, Category 6: almost all publishers consider collections of stories or even anthologies of stories, to be uncommercial and certain to lose them money.

This is a daunting prospect and seems to be entirely negative, yet there is a real lesson to be learned from this case study: adapt to your defined market and readers. Aim at this outlet, in every way, from style to format and research procedures.

High and low-brow

Arguably, one of the central notions behind this is related to the division between writing for its own sake, as aesthetic shaping and style, and mass-market readership. There is no reason why a writer cannot aim at both the course, but certainly, there is a clear division of markets in many sources of funding and organisation. A new writer can easily assess the nature of these markets by looking into some basic facts about publications and publishers:

➢ What is the circulation of the publication? (listed in *Writers' Handbook*).
➢ What editorial policy is openly stated?
➢ What is the funding source?
➢ What sort of values and objectives does the catalogue or advertising text promote?

An obvious example would be a magazine or anthology, or even a small publisher, financed by the Arts Council. The manager would have had to state an editorial policy in order to obtain the finance; for instance, the brief might be to publish only new writers under a certain age, or writers from a specific cultural heritage and so on. Or the brief might be to consider only 'innovative and experimental work', whatever that might mean.

Tutorial
Progress questions

1. What means are available for the writer to research a publishing outlet?
2. What does a new writer need most in a reference work?
3. List the main guidelines for submitting work in hard copy to an editor.

Points for discussion
1. Is there an argument for writing your work before considering a market for it? What might this be?

Practical assignments
1. Choose a publication or publisher in your range of writing interests. Write to them with a general enquiry about their lists and submission guidelines. They may even have promotional publications such as newsletters, which might be useful to you.
2. Compile a checklist of magazines and journals within one specified area, and then group or rank them according to their closeness to your style and treatments of subjects. Look closely at the typical tone, sentence structure, use of illustration and so on.

Study tips
1. Check out the information on professional societies in one of the two standard reference books mentioned in this chapter. Look for organisations within your area, and look at some publications produced by them. Try aiming at one of these with some writing; there will be no payments, but you will be testing the ground in a subject area within your specialism.
2. If you are attending a group or class, ask another student to be 'editor' and write a letter of enquiry describing what you

would like to submit. The feedback you receive should be simply whether or not your friend would like to see the submission, based on the 'pitch' in your letter.

****

7

Re-writing and Editing Your Work

One-minute summary: After looking at the process of selection, choice and submission of work, we return to the question of quality. We are now turning to consider the acquisition of positive and self-critical writing habits. The central skill here is handling the stages of writing from first tentative draft to the final typescript which you are happy to put in front of other professionals. The principles discussed here apply to writing in any category – even writing for performance poetry or prose, as every vocal delivery is still a finished text. There is also the notion that every text is always in flux anyway. As was mentioned in the first chapter, when is a work finished? The present focus is on the ways in which we can answer this question in more depth.

In this chapter, you will learn:

- ❑ How to enhance writing by television techniques.
- ❑ How to be more objectively self-critical.
- ❑ What factors determine re -writing.

Making your own standards

Standards are supposed to be general. Writers constantly talk and write about 'good' or even 'great' writing. People talk about everyday ways of telling what stories or books will be successful, and they often say that the criteria are that the reader 'can't put the book down' or that 'it's a real page-turner'. On academic courses, there are supposed to be criteria for what is *literary* and therefore 'quality' and worthy to be studied. But none of this helps the new writer, working alone on a typescript that grows with every writing session, and has the capacity to become an unwieldy monster rather than the cute little circumscribed piece you conceived of before you sat down to write.

A common question asked at writing events and courses is, 'How do I know when it's good enough'? The obvious answer is, good enough for what or for who? Partly, this is related to the account of identified markets examined in the previous chapter, but more profoundly, it is a matter of personal aims and standards. There appears to be categories of criteria with different writers, and these statements sum these up:

➢ It's spell-checked and grammar-checked. I can do no more.
➢ It's as good as that story by X in the last issue.
➢ I can't think of any other changes. Draft six will have to do.
➢ Well, Stephen King told this story better than I could ever do. There are even writers who constantly fret about 'what the editor might want' and they spend hours guessing and speculating about this.

Suggestions about criticism

Samuel Johnson memorably said that the way to think of a critic was that he may not be able to make a table, but hew a good table when he saw it. This is what is so hard for a writer to achieve: to be his or her own honest critic. Why is this? First, every critical judgement has a basis deep in some well-entrenched assumptions about 'good writing'. These should be ignored, because you have to know your own criteria, and apply them when you draft work or revise. Second, there are no universal criteria of excellence. Why else have best-sellers and future 'classics' been rejected by publishers? We all know stories of how many times *Watership Down* was rejected. At a talk, the poet George MacBeth said that his first collection was rejected twenty-eight times before it found a positive response.

What can a new writer do then, to cultivate the right attitude to drafting and revising? There are three areas of interest here:

a) *The functional level*

This is the language doctor process. You do the usual checks, but then read very closely for typos, clumsy expression and ambiguity. If your knowledge on this is shaky, invest in a style guide such as *Language Toolkit* edited by Jonathan Law, or a similar guide to English usage, just to sort out the difficulties with practice/practise pairs and split infinitives.

b) *The cohesion level*

Your concern here is for the integration of what you are writing. You need to be aware of questions about how the subject and style change and develop as the structure of the work goes on. Topics such as linking phrases and variety of sentences figure in this.

c) *The voice level*

The 'writer's voice' is the most illusive subject in creative writing. It means your sense of authenticity and uniqueness of your own writing style. This is easy to see in an extreme, very idiosyncratic writer but for most writing it is a place on a spectrum of a myriad different voices.

Making your own standards

Putting these areas of drafting together, it must be stressed that you have to develop your own sense of standards, and this only comes with the perfecting of your own treatment of the subject.

We now look more closely at these, and for this analysis we intend to use a short piece of poetry, simply because drafting and changing are easier to see with this type of writing. Here is draft one of the lyric:

Anglers
Sitting still, the anglers wait in a dream.

70

What are they thinking of?
Thoughts are tipped out like litter.
Or like the wriggling bait in their tins.
The wind is vacant. Nothing stirs around.
Sandpipers are calling across potato fields.
Like they fish in Lincolnshire,
I'm a jealous poet wanting great metaphors.

This is a first draft from a notebook. The aim is clearly to make a link between fishing and writing poems. It has an interesting heart to the writing, but it is clumsy and lacks a proper 'design'. The second draft was more to do with syntax and clarity than anything else:

Anglers
Silent, intent on their dream
Of a white-gold fin under them,
The angler tips out their thoughts
Like the wriggling bait
On the wet earth.

Vacancy drifts on the wind,
Past the hillock where pipers whoop.
I walk past the potato fields,
Lincolnshire pushing me into jealousy.
As I fish for metaphors
To beat the last one.

This was an improvement, but reading it aloud, it sounded like a mixture of Thomas Hardy and a pretentious voice that was not quite Stephen Wade. The final draft compressed all the ideas and made the metaphors integrate more clearly into the reflections of the poet watching the scene:

Anglers
Silent, intent on the dream
Of a white-gold flash beneath them,
The anglers tip their thoughts out

71

Like the wriggling bait
On the sodden dark earth.
Vacancy drifts on the wind,
Past the hillock where pipers whoop.
I walk past the potato fields,
Lincolnshire stillness pushing me,
And I'm jealous as I fish for
Metaphors to beat the last one.

There was a determined attempt here to try to play down the staginess of the poet watching the anglers, and making the metaphor too ambitious. But notice the changes, and how they relate to the three categories of revision:

a) Syntax simplified – as in the penultimate line.
b) Adjectives used to make the subjects more vivid (white/gold / sodden dark…).
c) Compression and directness put into the opening (first three lines). Remember the principle of tripartite structure.

Testing for quality

It may be seen from this example that there were some organising principles in my drafting methods:

Comparison with other writers who have influenced me.

A concern for compactness – no excess words.

A need to change the syntax for clarity and 'sound effect' when read aloud.

The last point is crucially important. If possible, read your work aloud, particularly after a certain amount is on paper. If you are writing poetry, this is obvious; but for prose it is just as important, as prose also has its rhythms and cohesion. Every piece of writing should be tested for the sense of integration and development from A o Z. This is why so many writers use the simple principles of repetition and variation at crucial stages of the piece. An example might be, in a short story:

Opening: Edinburgh is full of surprises, and today was no exception, as it provided John Dean with a shock.
Central variation: Shocks ere coming thick and fast now in this place of contradictions.
Closure: Loose ends were never to be tied up. Not here in this city. It always knotted the emotions, always surprised you when you were most complacent.
Notice how the unifying factor here is a pulse in the prose statements, an echoic set of statements, used to fix a tone of voice for the reader, and create a mental mood to match the setting of the fiction.

The sound and life of writing

As noted earlier in the chapter, an extreme style, full of noticeable trick or feature, can stand out, but not be an overall voice. For instance, definite articles might be omitted for effect, like this:
Tree was angular, high and brown. Weeds hung down, lianas touching earth like limbs calling for help. A man could have a few dangerous thoughts here. County was run-down and over-run at the same time.
Or, like Dylan Thomas, for instance, a voice can be insistently rhetorical, with no down-beat, even and mundane words or directness:
That the sum sanity might add to naught
And words fall crippled from the slaving lips,
Girls take to broomsticks when the thief of night
Has stolen the starved babies from their laps... (from 'Twelve')
Note how the voice I deliberately high, stylised and insistently intense.

In other words, testing for quality is a matter of verifying the voice you instinctively used when the thought transmuted into words. This is the authentic voice and it needs to be understood by you: no one else will be interested. Even a small adornment to style can change a whole feel of what the voice is, as in these two passages, when all that happens is that adverbs are added:

a) he entered, and it was a night for moving into the pool of light, where he could wait for her.

b) he entered stealthily. It was a night for silently moving, stepping mouse-like into the pool of light, where he could anxiously wait for her.

This shows that changing, adding or taking away small detail can change the dominant voice behind the writing.

Accessing the genuine voice

Your own genuine voice, then begins as what seems to be the instinctively correct voice of telling, showing or describing, but then passes through a spectrum of rewriting as you adjust to judgements, self-criticism and awareness of the readership or purpose – or even of general generic features. How can you pinpoint this process and so understand it?

This is the spectrum:

First pre-writing stage....draft one, instinctive....draft two, adjusted....draft three etc. revisions for suitability for others....final draft and reading....comparison of first and last drafts.

A practical way to work on this is to record yourself reading a passage as naturally as possible. As you play it back, compare it to the original impulse of the idea. This is what will happen:

Pre-writing: the plan in your head and the shaping patterns of the inner voice/then the opening, which sets the tone like a tuning-fork/then the attempts to maintain that tone throughout.

Recording this will highlight the uneasiness and the 'gear-changes' as you adjust the structure to changing events, awareness or market/readership factors. This is why there are so many well-documented examples of writers arguing with editors with regard to 'necessary changes' and why writers are so keen for images on the covers of their books to be accurate to the characters and setting in their story.

Tell the tale

Another simple strategy to access this authentic voice and how it adapts, is to tell an anecdote to a friend, with all the usual intonations, hesitancy and repetitions. The write the anecdote down as a short piece of narrative. Ask the friend to explain the difference in the effects of the two versions, and what their responses (or preferences) are. For instance, here is a story from a recorded anecdote used in a creative writing class:

In the bar like, typical Sunday afternoon you know like...full of couples eating a big lunch. Sunny day...bloke at the bar, just minding his own business like. In comes these bikers...Hell's Angels they were, all black leather and tattoos. Bloke at the bar wouldn't shift to make room for 'em...ruddy axe comes down on his wrist...chopped it off, chopped the ruddy hand off, you know, 'cos he didn't shift over for these lads...

Obviously, there is a realistic tone to this, but it's not loaded with artifice. The central question of narrative thus arises here: how far does a writer enhance and embellish that natural voice of each narrative? Should he or she do so at all? One answer is to write drama: then you can monopolise on these things; but many of us don't or can't write drama; we want to write prose or poetry, so the issue has a troublesome depth.

Selection and rejection

It is impossible to make a general statement about what to change and when, of course, but there are some general principles to guide a writer. First, ask some straight questions about any words you are doubtful about:

What is this word or phrase adding to the full work?
Am I doubtful because it is unconvincing in context?
Is it simply a weak expression, and so the thesaurus would help me?
Is the word or phrase moribund, flat, doing nothing to add interest?

As the piece develops, what happens is that, at each re-reading, you will want to erase words and add words. The drafting process emerges as habit of trusting your inner voice as you re-read and 'cut' or add. Doing this involves testing what you have against these criteria:

➢ Viability regarding 'real life'.
➢ Suitability for the genre or category.
➢ Closeness to the intended readership.
➢ Personal satisfaction – in line with your own aesthetic.

The plain answer to how to go about this process is simply, 'time will be the teacher'. Most writers would admit that this type of learning happens in the midst of a struggle to fine tune the writing until the 'feel' is right.

Tutorial

Practice questions

1. What do you now understand by 'voice' in writing?
2. Why is close re-reading essential, after computer checking?
3. What is meant by being a 'critic of your own work'?

Discussion points

1. What could be the difficulties involved in a writer insisting on trusting the first draft and not believing in close revision?
2. What might be the arguments in favour of collaborative writing?

Practical assignments

1. Look up some accounts of the writer-editor relationship in literary biographies. Think about what the relationship is, and what the communication process involved tells you about creative writing (examples would be found in the letters and biographies of D H Lawrence and Scott Fitzgerald).
2. Find some notebooks in print, such as those by Dylan Thomas (edited by Ralph Maud) and study how poems emerged from rough first drafts. Any full edition of the poems of Wilfred Owen will show changes made in lines of every poem. Complete editions of writers showing all changes made in drafts are called *variorum* editions.

8

Creative Non-Fiction

One-minute summary: starting out in creative writing for many people is not about writing fiction, despite the dominance of novels on the shelves. Other genres of factual writing have developed and have become increasingly popular. Factual writing covers life-writing, travel, documentary, reportage and the personal essay. To add more interest and possibilities for writers, there has been a cross-over tendency in these areas, so that it is common now to find books and articles that mix fact and fiction. Courses and journals in this area are proliferating, notably in the USA, and many courses in Britain contain tuition in writing biography and related areas. In this chapter we look at the skills involved in writing and researching some of these genres. In this chapter, you will learn:

➤ How to plan and research a non-fiction book
➤ How to mix genres and conventions
➤ What resources are available to you
➤ How original treatments of such subjects can be achieved

Life-writing
Creative non-fiction – what is it?

In America, there is a journal devoted to this writing, and the editor recently stressed the joy of writing in any form based on the real feel of life itself, and celebrated the nature of life is always as full of interest as the best conceived fictional plot. So creative non-fiction is a confluence of all the traditional forms of what used to be called 'discursive prose' – that is, reflective writing such as an essay, whether it is concerned with a place, a person, or a thought.

A cursory look at the book review columns or the shelves of a bookshop will indicate just how popular biography is. Today, there are many options and outlets for life-writing, as it is a genre that links to many other parallel forms of writing. Historically, the genre has developed from standard, factual and largely chronological accounts of famous lives into massive areas of writing and research with a growing stature in both the academy and in popular and mass-market publishing.

First, here is a summary of some of the options open to the biographer:

1. A scholarly, researched book or series of articles on important figures in a specific area.
2. Popular biography, less concerned with the context of a life than anecdotal bases of writing.
3. Profiles in short forms, or a related interview text.
4. Autobiography in the formal sense.
5. Crossover life-writing in which fact may be mixed with impressionable writing around the subject, or different time-references or viewpoints used.

There is also the relation of these categories to the different markets. For instance, not all biography may be of national interest, and the readership may be predominantly provincial, or for a special readership. This list of examples and brief descriptions will make the range of options and formats clear; books of these types have all been published in the last two years:

➢ A part imaginary life of a famous Victorian criminal.
➢ A monograph of a writer published for the 1890s Society.
➢ A new biography of a murderer with a polemic and a new theory about the identity of Jack the Ripper.
➢ An edited collection of journal extracts by a famous writer.

Even this list is not exhaustive. It leaves out life-writing produced for the children's market, and such things as academic books, like the series on British writers printed by the British Library.

This means that if life-writing is your aim, you have some serious thinking to do about which form and category is your version. The whole process of planning and putting together a synopsis for a biographical work is centred on the reason for writing. For instance, these are some of the well-established motives in writing biographies:

➤ To revise our view of the subject.
➤ To incorporate newly-discovered or available material.
➤ To pay due attention to a neglected personage.
➤ To help readers understand the work and achievement of the subject.
➤ To put forward a new theory about this particular life.

For example, supposing you wanted to write a life of Napoleon. There are perhaps several hundred in print, and in different languages. There would be a readership, but a publisher would need something original, in the treatment of the subject if not in the actual material. But if you realise that no-one has written a life of a figure of some importance in history, then your reasons may be easy to express.

A case study
A significant example of a biography that certainly needed to be written concerns the poet, Rupert Brooke. There was a cult of Brooke after his early death in Greece in the early part of the Great War. His poem, *The Soldier* had been read in Westminster Abbey; he was charming, noble and heroic. People bought his collected poems in great numbers for many years. There was eventually an official biography, written by Christopher Hassall, but a large amount of source material such as letters had been kept back in order not to stress the

unpleasant side of Brooke's nature. A biography published in 1998 used the previously unpublished material and a revisionary view of Brooke was available.

This example is very helpful to an aspiring life-writer. Think how interested a publisher would be if you had source material which was previously unknown. Such things do exist in university and in private libraries. They simply need to be located and a case made. The vogue of writing a life of someone in popular culture is a similar idea. You find a biography of the man who invented cat's eyes on the roads (Percy Shaw) and you wonder why that had never been written before. Well, someone had to think of it and do it. With real thought, a potentially successful idea is not so hard to find. Hunter Davies, for instance, had the simple but brilliant idea of writing about the lives of a group of people born in 1900 and published it at the Millennium.

Autobiography

Writing your own life is a different matter. Editors and publishers need a very good reason to be interested. Successful autobiographies tend to have a thread of real historical or sensational interest in the narrative, such as Eric Lomax's *The Railway Man*, about his part in building the Burmese Railway as a prisoner of war, or Frank McCourt's memoir of poverty and deprivation in Limerick, *Angela's Ashes*.

Of course, there are opportunities in local and provincial publishing. But there still needs to be a significant element, something more than simply a case of the writer thinking, 'Well, I fought in World War Two, so surely that would make an interesting book'? That writer would very soon find out that there are far too many books available which simply recount episodes in the conflict with Hitler already in print in dozens of standard historical works.

A life-writer interested in this sub-genre needs to consider these points:

1. *What novelty value do I have to offer? (A different angle on the narrative).*
2. *What is there in my treatment of the subject that will be striking for a reader?*
3. *In the content, what topics have not been approached by others?*
4. *Is there anything contemporary or even topical in my story?*

It can be seen from this summary that autobiography needs to have something special in one of these categories, so here is an example.

Idea

A work of autobiography, but interweaving three lives.

Elements of dreams and fantasies included in italics.

A confessional element, located in the author's experience of autism.

An account of the life of the author's parents' experience of the 1950s.

Treatment

Style to be almost fictional in quality but a 'feeling for fact' worked in – close detail to physical experience, sensual memory etc.

Genre

An experiment in life-writing, fusing fact and imagination, all around the experience of autism.

After this, it would essential to look for similar works, if any, and to note these, read them, and decide on your specific difference.

Place and Travel

This genre is another expression of creative non-fiction, and both types are undergoing similar changes to those in life-writing. Traditionally, travel writing was about interesting places, usually exotic or certainly places becoming popular with travellers. Writing about place was always rather lyrical and full of quasi-mystical reflections, such as we find in the writings of Llewelyn Powys, Richard Jefferies or Edward Thomas. But now there is again, a wider spectrum, with comic writing at one end (Tony Hawk's *Round Ireland with a Fridge*) to a celebration of a whole culture (Lisa St. Aubin de Teran's *Elements of Italy*).

Equally, writing about places is now possible on a very low budget. The genre takes in the challenge of writing about the familiar, so therefore the recent ideas in this area have been:

➤ *A tour of pubs with literary connections in Yorkshire.*
➤ *A book about Ilkley Moor and the story of its famous song.*
➤ *A celebration of mountains.*
➤ *A reference work about horses where famous music was written.*

This list hints at the diversity in this writing, but there are some broader considerations to deal with first. Writing about places just because they are not like home is not in itself sure to be interesting. The writer has to research first, to be aware of the dimensions of time, location and people; then a perspective needs to be selected before a writing treatment comes through. For instance, in a television programme in 2003, there was a feature on Greyfriar's Tower, a leaning tower in King's Lynn, Norfolk. It stands in the centre of the town often not noticed. It is currently fenced as there have been masonry falls. The tower was once part of a full Franciscan priory, a victim of the Dissolution of the monasteries under Henry VIII.

For a travel/place writer, the research might involve looking closer. This would reveal a stunning set of stone carvings high in the tower, and also to a clearer idea of what the build was when it was whole. As to the location and people, the documentary brought in children and teachers from the adjacent school, and filmed them using the tower as part of a maths exercise. It also did a *vox pop* around the town.

Finally, there had to be a topical or human-interest angle on the place. In this case, that was easily solved. It was a documentary about saving national treasures which are little known. There was to be a vote on which one of several places should be saved from ruin.

If you follow this three-stage thinking, any place has the potential to make an interesting narrative.

Photography as a guide

A helpful way into this is to consider what directs you when you visit a place and choose subjects for photographs. You might find a fascinating old building, but an image of that will be no more than an image to the person who has never visited the place but seen the picture.

A photographer therefore always prefers a human presence, preferably un-posed. A walk in the streets of New York, for instance, could easily give a writer a 'subject' as the place is packed with human life. You might be walking along Central Park; all the tourists want to shoot a picture of the horse-drawn carriages or the apartment blocks where celebrities live. But what about the little girl with a kitten on the steps of the Plaza Hotel?

With all this in mind, writing about place has real potential for publication now, and the market is diverse. Here are some common publishing varieties:

➢ Travel articles with copious photographs for weekend supplements and 'glossies'.
➢ More investigative pieces with a political edge.
➢ Reportage: a genre dealing with immediately topical subjects.
➢ Substantial essays for paperbacks and journals such as *Granta* or *Witness*.

Discursive prose

You may not have a specialism in this area, but you enjoy producing non-fiction. This is not so rare. Many prose forms of writing are not governed by considerations of genre, and after all, a genre is just a name. If a reader loves a book, what does the genre tag matter? A well-established example of this is the essay. Now, the essay has along pedigree, and it is possible to follow its history very clearly:

In the eighteenth century, the first periodicals for the essay, *The Spectator* and *The Tatler*, provided a market for literary men with no academic expertise but a 'wide culture'.

By the Victorian period, more substantial essays on very serious political, literary and historical subjects developed, but alongside more humorous and journalistic pieces. For instance, Charles Lamb's *Essays of Elia* (1823) are impressionistic, personal and reflective, whereas Macaulay's essays written for the *Edinburgh Review* from 1825 onwards were lengthy and authoritative.

In the age of the new commuters, notably in the years c. 1890 – 1930, the short entertaining essay emerged, in the hand of G K Chesterton, E V Lucas and J B Priestley.

Today we have survivals of the third phase in the weeklies and monthlies, such as *The Spectator, The Oldie* and *Prospect*.

Give me three subjects...

The central form of discursive prose, known as *belleslettres*, formerly had a reputation for being hastily written, opinionated and trivial. But that was the point of it; it was said that Priestley could be given twenty minutes and he could write you an essay on a lamb chop, a suit and a bomb (or any other randomly selected topics). That was the whole idea of the essay – to entertain and to present a vibrant or eccentric personality.

If you want to write in any of these versions of the essay, you need to mix (and most successfully), these elements:

A projection of personality
A topical theme
A device such as an invented persona or place
On-going details as sources of humour

    Bridget Jones's Diary started as a column, and the column is perhaps the closest thing we have to the Chestertonian essay. A worthwhile first step in this writing is to approach your local paper. You would have small chance of competing with names such as Alan Coren or Miles Kingston in the daily national papers, but being in print is the first step.

Advice from the professionals

Editors of feature articles for the nationals and the magazines usually itemise these points when asked what they are looking for in creative non-fiction:

➢ A submission from someone already published on a small scale (local publications, student magazines etc.).

➢ A writing style close to the middle ground of their publication.

➢ Individuality, mixing information with entertainment.

There are also some obvious do-not points, such as do not simply list facts in these genres. A paragraph like this belongs in a school textbook or an academic journal:

    Let us remind ourselves of some facts about Lincoln. Abraham Lincoln was the sixteenth President of the USA. He lived from 1809 to 1865. He saved the Union, freed the slaves, and was the staunchest defender of democracy.

Mixing genres

Today, a writer has the great advantage of being free of any reductive definition of a 'genre', and publishers expect conventions and forms to be mixed, in any interesting prose style. A typical example would be Bill Bryson, who could be labelled as a travel writer, but has, in fact, produced a boom on the English language in America and a history of 'just about everything'. This type of humour and almost whimsical mixtures of topics and styles has been a wonderful release for the creative writer.

You can easily dabble with these styles in your notebook. For example, you can write about an interesting subject in three different ways, in three distinct voices. A very good example of this blurring of narrative conventions is in a novel I mentioned earlier, *Flaubert's Parrot* by Julian Barnes. A short summary of what he fuses would give us this:

A fictional framework using a narrator, Geoffrey, a doctor.
The story of Flaubert's life told by theme rather than chronology.
Passages of literary criticism in which he quotes well-known academics.
Essay-style digressions on any passing subject.

There would be nothing to stop a prose-writer today developing a long work by writing two alternating styles, one fictional narration and the other the 'author's voice'. In fact, there is a long tradition of fiction with an author's presence in the text, as when Charlotte Brontë breaks off from her novel to say, 'Dear reader …'.

As always, the successful factor here is the pre-writing phase: planning, research and sheer hard thinking. Nothing is so disheartening as being well into a writing project only to discover that someone has already written your book, and better than you feel you could ever write it. Do the meticulous planning before this situation can ever arise.

Tutorial
Practice questions
1. What makes creative non-fiction so difficult to define?

2. What has been the main change in the way we perceive literary genres since 'literature' became a subject to be studied?

Discussion points

What factors might need to be considered if you were setting out to write a biography of a person whose life was already written, but not in a definitive and official form?

Practical assignments

1. Research the life of a local person who has been involved in any major international or national events (local politicians perhaps or charity-workers). List what is actually in print, and devise your argument for a book proposal to a publisher.

2. Consider what make a biography 'topical'. You might scan the shelves of the local bookshop, read the cover-blurbs and see if the sales talk relates to any contemporary 'hook' for the appeal to the buyer.

Study tips

1. Find two essays in the creative non-fiction genre. Choose one from the early twentieth century (Chesterton, Lucas, Belloc etc.) and one form a column in a quality daily paper (because these are longer than average). Look at what has changed in terms of the vocabulary, type of social reference, and the presence of the author's personality in the text.

2. Draft a short piece (say 1000 words) mildly or humorously sending up a current local issue. Try out the editor of the local paper with this. Use the form of a letter but extend it into a mock argument. Irony and sarcasm are often found in the essay genre (examples today would be in the essays of Terry Jones or Arthur Marshall).

****

9

Starting out in Fiction

One-minute summary: There is an abundance of advice on writing fiction in print, so this chapter is purposely a summary of the essential nature and components of fiction in print. For that reason, here we survey the principal aspects of narrative that will have to feature in what you do; then there is a focus on the short story. Attention is also given to some of the theory and speculation behind the story itself, in any form. Again, there will be only minimal attention given to revising, as that has been dealt with previously. We go on to consider what skills help to build the structure of a story, and how writers and editors tend to work on such elusive concepts as 'tone' and 'pace'.

In this chapter, you will learn:

➤ What factors constitute fictional interest.
➤ How writers develop material into narrative.
➤ What part plot and character play in this process.
➤ How successful story deals with themes and ideas.

The nature of narrative

Most writers think they know how to tell a story. Most writers also think they know a good 'kernel' of a story when they meet one. If that is true, why are there so many thousands of aspiring novelists who have failed to impress editors, and whose work lies in desk-drawers, unread? One answer is that storytelling is a very sophisticated and skilful art, sometimes simple on the surface, but very difficult to write well. Even the shortest story has to have certain key elements, and these are not always straightforward skills, open to plain explanation.

Think about how you and other people tell jokes or recount anecdotes from personal experience. Some tell the tale fluently, seamlessly, and listeners laugh and respond. Others stumble, forget elements of the story, and lose the interest and 'flow' of the experience.

➢ This is not always a guide to who might be the best writer. Many writers tell a marvellous story in print but cannot interest people when they tell jokes. Therefore, there must be some aspects of fiction-writing which are key concepts. We could start with these:

➢ A direct or implied rapport between writer and reader (via a narrator sometimes).

➢ A shared sense of reality or imagination (or both).

➢ A 'willing suspension of disbelief' as the story unfolds.

➢ Accessible and authentic language.

➢ Convincing expression of feelings/emotions/thoughts.

➢ An invented world of irresistible appeal.

Note the central importance of the 'willing suspension of disbelief', a phrase coined by Samuel Taylor Coleridge. It is that unspoken agreement between teller and listener that this time and space in their lives is set aside of a story – a shared indulgence in that imagined world. It is exactly the same thing as the condition of the mind as we enter a theatre. As the play starts, actors and audience are tacitly accepting that this world *could* exist and these things, however unlikely, *might* happen somewhere.

The appeal of standing outside time

An old phrase used about stories, that they keep old and young alike 'in the chimney corner' reminds us that oral storytelling was the first variety. In this version of fiction, the teller sees the reactions of the listener. If you have read a child a bedtime story, you have the same thing: you see from the child's face what responses the story is creating. Children even question the logic of stories, or want to respond to the moral issues raised. Obviously, they show happiness and fear more explicitly than most adults. If you want to think about the fundamental nature of fiction, tell a child a story.

The point is, we all desperately want stories. Our lives are a bundle of narratives anyway, and the individual life itself is a parallel concept to an imagined fictional world. Think about some of the basic patterns of the great stories, like a tragedy for instance:

Classical tragedy

Phase one: The hero has an outstanding quality of character.

He or she rises to attain some position or satisfaction.

Phase two: But something deep in the personality is the worm in the apple.

A crack appears, a weakness shows.Maybe an external threat arrives.

Phase three: The hero falls inevitably to their doom.

As Aristotle rightly said, we feel pity and fear at such a story, because the protagonists are **like us but not o us.** That is, reading fiction, the reader wants to identify with the person and situation but not too much. Think of two people discussing a murder story in the press. One will recount it, and the other will respond, usually expressed horror and sympathy. But there is a distance, an *aesthetic distance*. This distance is where writers place their narrative effects.

The idea of *person*

We cannot go into great depth here, but if you are new to writing fiction, then consider the simple device of using a different person (a grammatical term) to tell a story. In grammar, these are examples:

First person singular – I, me, my   First person
plural – We, our(s)
Second person singular – He, she, it, its   Second
person plural – You, your(s)
Third person singular – He, she, it, its   Third
person plural – They, their(s)

Who tells the story is therefore crucially important. Look at this contrast:

First person:

The name's John Bentley. I'm an apprentice engineer in Leeds. It's boring stuff, and I've had my fill of it. Too many bosses you see. I want out, and I want out now.

Third person:

John Bentley was an apprentice engineer. He was finding the work in his Leeds factory tedious and unrewarding. He wanted to leave.

The differences are obvious. The first person takes you closer, involves you, the reader. The third person creates distance. Both can be effective narration methods. The second person, using 'you' is hard to sustain but can be used, as in 'You know the kind of thing that happens when you walk into a shop and find there's a fire alarm in progress'? But in most cases, fiction involves either mixtures of these, or one dominant method, in most cases first or third person.

The short story

There are many good reasons why writing a short story is an ideal way to start honing your skills as a storyteller. Perhaps it might be more useful to use the term 'short fiction', as today there is a wider spectrum of possibilities. This is because not all short stories have a 'story' in the sense of a strong spine of plot and events. Many short fictions are little more than impressionistic insights into a moment of being or experience. They can often be about the condition of living rather than events in the 'life' of the central character.

A constructive way to understand the idea of a short story is to think about how a story usually focuses on a circumscribed event or period of time within an imagined life:

Story span or focus

_____/

/_____

Imagined life

Note how a story not only deals with a significant event or confrontation; it also asks the reader to 'fill in' the rest of the character's imagined life. Techniques such as flashbacks or innovative narration methods can help the reader to anticipate or imagine details. Supposing sentences like this are added, for instance:

John had known awkward situations like this before, when he had been at boarding school and met bullies.

This invites the reader to apply assumptions and pre-conceptions about boarding schools and bullies, and so to be actively involved with the story imaginatively.

In contrast, the traditional realist novel, such as Dicken's *Great Expectations*, often deals with a 'life' chronologically told:

Birth and education   marriage   formative influences   resolution

Oppositions

Most guides to fiction generally and short stories in particular emphasise the idea of conflict. A more useful way of thinking about this might be to use the notion of oppositions. Many stories are developed around these 'turning points' in a life for example:

➢ A crucial encounter.
➢ A sudden reversal of fortune.
➢ Radical self-realisation.
➢ A powerful emotion now realised.
➢ A moment of extreme fear/love/guilt etc.

Note how you can write into the heart of such storylines a distinct opposition. All a story needs is an obstacle in the way of fulfilment, an enemy, or an inner uncertainty, and there is an opposition. As many classic stories show, the event dealt with need not be massively world-changing: simply important in the world of the character and setting. For instance, take short stories set in war; the opposition is already there on a grand scale, so the writer needs to add another conflict, perhaps an inner, personal one such as a soldier's guilt at something he did 'back home' and you have a dual layer of fictional interest.

Plot and character

This brings us to the question of the logistics of putting together a compelling story. There tend to be two broad ways of working:

Writer 1:Plenty of thought given to working out a plot, even down to a series of 'events' and then the invention of the key turning points and the creation of a resolution in the closure.
This is plot-driven.
Writer 2:
The stress here is on inventing a character; some writers try methods like creating an imaginary CV for their person. They work out typical clothes and speech habits, and so on. Some writers work from photographs of people who match their mental conceptions of the character.
This is essential empathic.

It might be a case of being so deeply 'inside' the mind and feelings of the character that you can write directly from the empathic emotions: the writer 'is' the character, and the plot comes along from this creation. But it helps if, whichever way you write, you ask some questions first and work them out in the notebook:

What is the essential situation?
What does the character want?
Why does the character act or think in this way?
What is to be achieved?
What stands in the way of this achievement?

Some writers spend hours working out the human nature behind certain key motivations, and this can pay off. For example, supposing your story is essentially about jealousy.

You might look closely into how a person thinks and behaves when jealous, going deeper than the obvious surface features of behaviour. You might borrow ideas from classic literary treatments of the subject, such as Shakespeare's *Othello*.

Template stories

This brings up the idea of creating short stories from narratives already in existence. The retelling and up-dating of old tales, myths and parables is an interesting way to deal with plots. Supposing you told the story of *The Good Samaritan* but set it in New York in 2003? Think how you could transpose people, settings and beliefs, to say nothing of the moral theme under the story.

Myths and fables have another advantage: they have ready-made plots with powerful confrontations, oppositions and turning points. You might want to deal with one of the commonest themes in short fiction: the idea of an *epiphany*. This is a story in which a truth or realisation is revealed to a character, such as in many tragic myths and epics in which a character suddenly finds out a terrible truth (the Oedipus myth, for instance, where Oedipus finds out that he has unwittingly killed his father and married his mother).

A worthwhile way to work on short story skills is to re-tell an old story, giving your character an epiphany on a much more mundane level, like a woman finding out that the rich sister who went to Australia all those years ago has been living a lie: she has been very unhappy for years, yet writing letters telling everyone how fulfilled and joyful she is in her new life. Just one key incident is needed to bring about the epiphany in the sister in England, when she learns the truth, or the sister in Australia, when she is forced to speak the truth.

A template story can also be suitable for humour and satire. They are potentially useful for writing something with an ironic theme. Take the example of Monty Python's *Life of Brian* for instance, or a famous short story by Nikolai Gogol,

The Nose, which is about a barber who finds a nose one day in his bread. Bizarre as this sounds, it is not a grotesque story as ridiculous as a surreal narrative, but a story about ambition and snobbery.

Structure and theme

It is possible to produce a story from a 'theme' – that is, in order to demonstrate a view of society, for instance, but the result would be limited to something in the category of 'the literature of ideas', in other words, successful stories more often emerge from an instinctive drive to express something centred on a focal character and place than on an abstraction.

However, there are plenty of examples of collections of stories grouped according to a layering or interplay of themes: an example would be James Joyce's collection, *Dubliners* (1914) in which he puts forward an account of a community in the grip of various versions of 'moral paralysis'. The point is, if you do like working from a theme, you need to decide how far to go with literary deliberateness and planning. For instance, suppose you want to write a story about small lives and ordinary people in a great city. You could easily think like this:

Place: a massive concrete jungle, tower-block and anonymity. A place without a neighbourhood or proper sense of community.

Characters: Jimmy and rose, young, married couple trying to make a future and build their careers.

Obstacles: A lack of real friendships and a sense of isolation. They are hemmed in by a neighbourhood working mainly through criminal activities.

Observe how deliberate this is. It is much better to use one central symbolic or representative feature like a building or a road to define the environment; the best stories work from a human centre, fired by the writer's emotional commitment to the invented people and the motivations explored.

What is meant by structure?

Edgar Allan Poe saw the short story as a 'single action' essentially, and not many stories take on parallel plots or more than two important characters, so in most cases, what is called structure is a matter of maintaining what you started in the establishing narrative voice of your story.

Theories about how stories of different types tend to have a theoretical basis abound; most handbooks talk about working by various structural principles. Plots and structures are often called 'circular' or 'rise-fall-rise', and so on, as the structures use patterns of events towards the resolution. Often, diagrams are used, or metaphors like the notion of a story being structured like a Russian Doll – the writer taking one layer off at a time, revealing yet another area of interest, until the centre is reached.

Some of these are worthwhile, but a story succeeds or fails on the way in which the central spine of the narrative develops through stages. Writers often have different name for these processes. Here are some you could experiment with:

1. Plant for Winter
As the phrase implies, the technique is to set up a significant central event early on, with no real clue as to what the 'harvest' will be at the closure.

2. Motif
This is where a story can be developed around things such as objects, possessions or small details. You might look at Gogol's *The Overcoat* as an example. The approach is to make an object or image indicate something fundamental about the people and society around it.

3. Turning Points
Here, the aim is to have a series of stages towards the closure, and at each stage to have a 'cliff-hanger' – something momentous but not final. A typical example would be the 'two strangers meet on a train' story; the whole story is dependent

on the conversation and its twists and turns, until something really significant or ironical closes the scene.

Structure often emerges naturally, in that a story is often written at one sitting, and so the rhythm and tone of voice are easily maintained. If a writer does not leave a story for several hours and then come back to it, the continuity and sense of the narrative being smoothly integrated is kept. So structure becomes a matter of the writer learning by habit how to do the following, and when to shift from one stage to the other:

Phase one: *Establish character, place, time etc., as required.*
Phase two: *Create a clear sense of motivation.*
Phase three: *Show the obstacles/oppositional factors.*
Phase four: *Resolve or create a satisfactory closure.*

Finally, it may be that your definition of what part structure and theme play in your story will always be secondary to the narrative voice. A good place to see the sheer dynamism of a dominant and persuasive tone of voice is in the stories of the American writer, John Cheever, who made the short story his specialism. His stories illustrate the dictum that if you believe in your characters, then the reader will. If you can create an authentic voice and maintain it convincingly, you will succeed in this difficult art.

Tutorial
Progress questions
1. What is the link between oral tales and literary, written narrative?
2. Why is awareness of the reader such an important factor?
3. What is meant by 'the willing suspension of disbelief'?

Points for discussion
What can be learned about writing fiction from other narrative media such as film or radio? Consider how open other forms are to experiment and innovation.

Practical assignments

1. Choose a classic short story with a twist in the tale and assess its structure and plot in terms of how it sets up the crisis in its characterisation. Maupassant's *The Necklace* is a perfect example.
2. Compare other short forms of story-telling to the short story itself (the one-act play, the ballad song and so on) and think about similarities and differences. What might the prose fiction writer learn from these parallel forms and conventions?

Study tips

1. When you develop a story idea in a notebook, try to express the whole plot in its minimal for, say 200 words. Then expand from that. This exercise tends to clarify the important elements and leave out the less interesting ones.
2. Find reflections on fiction-writing in interviews with novelists, and do a check-list of different research and writing methods. Particularly interesting are the attitudes of novelists to short stories. Some see them as sprints compared to a marathon; others see them as shrunk novels.

****

10

Writing for Performance

One-minute summary: Although some areas of writing have had to be omitted here for reasons of space and scope, a summary of possibilities for dramatic writing is given here, covering writing comedy, short drama and performance poetry. The stress in this final chapter is on three main topic areas: performance in its many guises; humour and potential collaborative writing. There is a survey of options open to a new writer, an account of support and information sources, and essential methods and approaches are discussed.

In this chapter, you will learn:

➤ How to place your writing in the spectrum of performance possibilities.

➤ How dramatic writing can be produced, researched and submitted.

➤ What factors can help in working with others.

Patter, comedy and sketch

New writers may be astonished to learn that there is a constant demand for original comedy writing; the television channels are burning to find the next original sitcom to match *Father Ted* or *Only Fools and Horses.* But there is also a demand for every form of short comic writing, from one-liners to sketches (often to fit in an already winning format such as *The Sketch Show*, and also material for stage presentation. There are two large comedy-writing organisations, both aiming to provide members with contacts such as agents and other writers to work with, as well as providing workshops and conferences. But what is the nature of comedy? It is as difficult to define as tragedy or melodrama. It is no enough to say 'something that makes you laugh' as the sense of humour notoriously shifts with cultural context, changing morals, and new perceptions about relationships.

But it is possible to start with some versions of the sources that can create a comic vision:

The sense of the absurd.

Reversion of the logical to the illogical.

Ridicule and abuse/satire.

Irony and sarcasm.

The comedy of the individual/eccentricity.

What is often not acknowledged fully is the closeness of a laugh to weeping. In an episode of One Foot in the Grave, Meldrew and friends are first lost in a wilderness, hen Victor stumbles upon a residential home for old people in which residents are barbarously abused. Yet this is in the comedy genre. Laughter has a safety valve aspect, and laughs often come from the syndrome of 'there but for the grace of God go I...' The humour of death is thus a mix of relief and our sense of incomprehension. What we do not understand we fear, and if we fear, we find a space to laugh in.

So for many writers, producing humour means relying on the individual sense of the absurd or ridiculous, running with that, and eventually testing it out. The cartoonist Gary Larson clearly sees profound humour in many of the stereotypes of American life, but it may not be everyone who shares his love of speaking cows, overweight teenagers and chickens taking to petty crime. A writer has to start with the humour inside, already there, latent but in need of a voice. If you want to entertain others, first entertain yourself. For many, starting with aimless patter is the way to create the voice of the comic attitude or persona. Just as a listener can immediately tell Billy Connolly or Rab C Nesbit, so the flow of voice entrenched in your own brand of humour can open up more sustained writing.

For example, here is some 'patter' based on a character who is a die-hard opinionated Yorkshireman from a bygone era:

Well, our Bessie were houseproud all right She hovered every hour on the hour. I had to lift me legs up so often I belly muscles like steel. Mind you she were a bit slow. I once had her playing marbles
with sheep's droppings. She were very religious mind…very odd. She
were the only member of the Plymouth Brethren what lived in Batley…
It were a long walk to church on a Sunday…

A useful way of working is to establish this humorous creation of voice first, fill in the cultural reference, then work through these stages, to see how far it goes:

Phase one: Continue the patter until you have some pages of notes. Broaden the writing into dialogue.
Shape this into a short sketch.
Decide on re-drafting what to add in terms of setting, actions, clothes etc.

After all, a sketch is one minute action with a coming-together of several potentially humorous elements. Take a typical sketch from radio humour for instance.

Situation - A man has a lorry load of wood to deliver to London.

Humour – his voice, attitude, sound effects, absurdity.

He drives down the A1 asking questions. He repeats the line: I have to deliver this Lot, so is this the road to London.

Next he arrives in Manchester. He asks the same question.

Finally, on Westminster Bridge he stops and asks the same question. When told 'It's Westminster Bridge' he swears, turns round and says he'll never find 'ruddy London…'

The humour comes from (a) his accent (make him a Northerner) and (b) his lack of knowledge (country bumpkin).

What this outline does not show is the *treatment*. Everything lies in that.

Treatment

Imagine you have to explain a funny idea. As soon as you do this, and prepare a synopsis to submit to a television or radio producer, you sense the heart of the comedy slip away. This is a clue to the best way to express a treatment of a comic idea. For instance, a man with colour prejudice is not funny. He is hateful to all civilised people. But make him a harmless monster, a massive and overstated version of a tiny trait in many people and you have Alf Garnett. If you had to explain the comic treatment of Garnett you could put these things in your proposal or synopsis of your idea:

1. The cultural context: West Ham United, topical political humour (he is rabid Tory).
2. The monster. He lacks any form of humour except ridicule and sarcasm. So the writer makes him the butt of the same things.
3. The other characters: all easy to identify with – more exemplary in terms of ordinariness. 'Like us' thinks the viewer.
4. Appearance, traits. Garnett is extreme and loud. His London accent and patriotic habits are projected as if he is a throwback, a parody of himself, as presented.

The writer, Johnny Speight, had a winner, because he was clear of three things:
The thin edge between absurdity and monstrosity.
'Englishness' as a problem but also as quaint.
The tendency for people to laugh at figures like 'Punch'.
In fact, some of the roots of that humour is in the appeal of *Punch and Judy* and traditional pantomime. So even the stage treatment, the style and language, were part of the comic subject.

Development of dialogue

Supposing you have the comic vision and then you have worked on the voice and the character. The next step is the fundamental skill of dramatic writing: authentic dialogue. Harold Pinter said that when he started writing, as long as he had two people in a room and they could start talking convincingly, he had a chance of a play, of some dramatic interchange. In comedy, if you differentiate between characters very clearly, you have a basic for humour. A useful way to start is to see what opposites, what conflicts, fit your scenario. It could be one of these:

Old and young.

Innocent and corrupt.

Eccentric and conformist.

Prisoner and warder.

And so on, into the social world where opposites create stories.

If you have one strong character, a Garnett, a Hancock or a Del Boy, other characters have to be foils and sounding-boards, finely distinguished. Simple techniques like ridicule can bring this out:

Dave; Hey Pete…how come your shorts are always clean as a whistle every Sunday?

Pete: Well, a player should be well turned out.

Dave: I see, like your Doreen turned you out, out of bed without getting your oats.

Pete: Do you have to turn everything dirty?

Dave: No, the pitch'll do that for me mate.

Probably more so than in prose fiction, dramatic humour tends to run with the talk, he talk generating more talk, as the writer trusts in their 'ear' for the sense of the genuine character.

It is easier to say what should not be done in dialogue than what should be done:

> ➤ Be careful not to make dialogue too informative, too loaded with facts.
> ➤ Leave out anything that does not serve a purpose 9why would Jim and Pat talk about the weather? Is it funny?)
> ➤ Cut out digressions and explanations to the shortest form possible.
> ➤ Let one statement lead smoothly to another.
> ➤ Use the natural rhythms of speech, trust your own ear for reality.

Radio drama or fiction

Some of the most challenging and rewarding openings exist in these media. After all, the nature of the audience dictates a very specific approach to writing. Although there is a genuine diversity of forms and conventions in writing for radio, there are certain set forms that are ideal for practising the demands of the medium. Traditionally, these have been the varieties of scripts available and in demand:

Talks

Short stories

Monologues

Short drama

Sitcom

Experimental writing (ie narrative verse)

As an accessible and interesting way into writing for radio, the monologue has much appeal. A monologue is literally 'one voice' speaking. Normally, it takes the form of a single voice pinned to a specific moment, emotion or situation, as in the very successful series of *Talking heads* by Alan Bennett. But there are other varieties:

The situational: *One person locked into a certain setting such as a moment before an important interview.*

The assumed listener: *Here, the writer as another character whom the speaker addresses, and therefore, the listener feels present almost as someone eavesdropping.*

Detached voice/voices: A monologue can be used more poetically, as in T S Eliot's great poem, The Waste Land (1922).

The first variety is the most generally appealing, as one character fills the entire story; we feel that the person talking, confiding or even confessing to us, each individual listener, as in this short extract:

> *Well I don't know why he brought me here. I mean it's the end of Land as we know it…Spurn Point. We can be alone, he said, I have something very pressing to say to you, he said. I hope he's not going to pop the question, not on Spurn Point, miles further on from Hull. I mean, imagine the headline, Spurned on Spurn Point…*

A monologue tends to be an ideal opening challenge, as the established voice carries the writer through quite confidently. The only problem is, you need shape, it is very tempting to ramble on and not have a structure. The secret of success is not to have a deliberate, visible structure, but to close the piece in ways that either resolve or at least bring together the various subjects covered throughout. If your character is waiting for that interview, it can end with them being called into the room; or it can end with the voice fading into uncertainty.

Stories on the air

With fiction written specifically for radio, obviously, the writer needs to work with different aspects of the craft made more prominent than they would normally be:

A more prominent use of dialogue

More imagined or evoked milieu

Greater use of 'sound picture' in establishing place

Possibility of time manipulation being important – used with music and sound effects.

Stories for radio tend to do well when the subject is large-scale and can involve cuts from the interior life to the world of public events, or conversely, when the narrator evokes an intense selfhood, a directing consciousness from which we the listeners are brought into the responses very intimately.

One-act plays

This is genre that has always had a minority appeal, and has a clear value for a small theatre company looking for amateur production on a manageable scale. It seems that the most viable way to start writing short drama is to approach one of the hundreds of theatre companies who advertise in the writing journals for new scripts. Magazines such as *Writers' Forum* regularly feature prizes offered for new play-writing, and local festivals often have a similar open competition. There are some obvious steps to take here:

Read examples in play collections (mainly published by Samuel French or Nick Hern Books).

Learn the adaptations of short story principles to stage form: the importance of action and expression and above all the interplay of mixed voices.

Practise by writing prose narrative first, then translating into dialogue.

Traditionally, one-act plays deal with a single situation, intensely recounted, with a 'tight focus', that is, often with one manageable piece of material either in a single relationship or with a small group of say six people. This is why comedy works so well in this context. But other possibilities are:

➢ The epiphany story (as discussed in the short stories section).

➢ The mysterious encounter.

➢ The psychological drama (a person has done something radical).

➢ Twist in the tail story.

In other words, like short stories, you can put the emphasis on plot or character, but above all, the situation you make has to have optimum dramatic interest. Most playwrights either start with this form, or take an interest in its demand for a compact structure and a focus on a single event. A typical example

106

would be Anton Chekhov, who wrote many short stories and full-length plays, but who was drawn to the one-act play because it gave him the chance to use the short story structure but add a poetic, lyrical dimension, and use his sense of place alongside a personal vision more productively.

Drama and its special demands

From this wide range of examples it can be seen that writing for performance when there is a need for a story to be told demands a basic fabric of writing that adheres to the question about what makes a situation dramatic, as opposed to purely narrative?

Some answers might be:

The audience involvement is on a different level of imagination: they have visual prompts and guides.

The writer can orchestrate a variety of effects and senses in making the characters 'live' before us.

The humour, pathos and relationships are naturally more immediate. There is no way we the audience can follow the stage directions. We have to watch the actor.

For all these reasons, writing drama asks that the writer adds several dimensions to the writing. A visual and auditory level is added to the imaginative vision the writer had before the idea took shape in words. Writing drama, you have to work on the bringing together of action, voice, visual appeal and sounds. The authenticity comes with the successful confluence of these. So a one-act play is a notably appealing way to try out this difficult challenge on a small scale. The writer can simplify many aspects of the story to help make it a more manageable task. For example, the action can be two characters on a park bench (as in Edward Albee's famous play, *Zoo Story*) or one character and a pile of rubbish (as in Samuel Beckett's *Endgame*).

Specialist help is needed, though, for this writing. Arguably, more than any other genre, the dramatist needs others: a stage workshop, a group of friends, and at the very least a reading of the play or a studio performance. As with so much in creative writing, the best advice is to start on your doorstep; contact local drama groups or colleges.

Poetry and stand-up

In recent years, there has been a boom in performance poetry. Clubs and pubs hold 'poetry slams' and there has been an exciting development of poetic writing being used as part of a multi-media art-form.. At such occasions as the Edinburgh Festival, the Fringe opens up all kinds of opportunities for experimental performance poetry, and there is a wide variety of possibilities.

Poetry in its origins was always read aloud; Chaucer at the court of his king, Richard II would recite his poems, giving dramatic feeling and life to the descriptions and the dialogue. Years ago children were taught to recite stirring narrative poems such as Alfred Noyes's *The Highwayman* because poetry was seen as a public art. In the Victorian and Edwardian periods, for instance, poets were expected to be adept at delivering a 'reading' of their work very different from the more typical modern reading, in which poems of a more personal, interior nature are read and explained.

But writing for performance in this context is exciting and full of experimental potential. Consider the range of performance poets and their styles:

John Cooper Clarke: Punk Rock Mancunian humour and satire, with music.

John Hegley: low-key, absurd humour, poetry and song mixed.

Ian MacMillan: Yorkshire daftness, once part of a mobile play of voices outfit called the Circus of Poets.

Benjamin Zephaniah: Rasta and social comment with the speech-rhythms of talk and conversation at full stretch.

It is so hard to define, that some of it is stand-up comedy, and in many ways performers like Ian MacMillan are more stand-up comics than poets at some of their readings, depending on where they wish to place the emphasis.

Starting out

A sensible way to start is to think about the version you wish to produce, and here some differentiations and descriptions might help For instance:

Case study 1 – The Mersey Poets

In the 1960s a group of Liverpool poets became centre-stage in poetry. Roger McGough, Adrian Henri and Brian Patten. They 'read' their work, perhaps not actually 'performing' it, although they gave many of these, on stage, and often with music on the programme as well. Yet Roger McGough does not consider what does to be performance poetry. What he does is project with emotion and powerful intonation. He does sometimes 'act' the voice of a person in a poem, so he brings the poem to life; but he would debate the fact that some critics and writers think he is a performance poet.

Case study 2 – John Hegley

Conversely, John Hegley definitely performs his writing, in the sense that he moves a lot, uses projected expressions of humour, and gives full entertaining life to lyrics that would seem 'thin' on the page. He obviously conceives of a performance as a full, planned and integrated presentation, with interest generated at many levels.

All this helps a writer trying to write for performance. For instance, you might want to build the writing around an invented character, or use different voices.

Collaboration

This is where the idea of working with other writers becomes important. In any performative art form, a mix of voices will always add interest. Even a touring performance of storytelling with two actors will have extra interest from the contrast of voices. There are many different ways in which you can write in this way for performance purposes:

➤ Divide the labour – one writing dialogue and one narrative.

➤ Research/production – you might have one writer who enjoys the research, pre-writing stage.

➤ Bouncing off ideas – look at partnerships such as Galton and Simpson (who wrote for Hancock and for Eric Morecambe); they would talk through the lines, improving the responses, working on character for hours.

➤ Feeding of a personality – one writer might 'be' the character and the other works at forcing a response.

In all these strategies for working together, the advantage is that whenever there is a lull or an obstacle, you have two minds, tow imaginations, and a joint will to succeed.

Tutorial
Practice questions
1. Why is comedy so hard to define? Give some examples.
2. Why is so-called 'dark' comedy always elusive when critics try to explain its appeal?
3. What extra challenge is there for the storyteller in writing for a radio audience?

Discussion points
Is a monologue necessarily always fixed in a cultural setting or essentially comic, or does it have other possibilities?

Practical assignments
1. Find some monologues written within the text of full-length plays and ask yourself how these add to the overall design of the dramatic structure. Good examples would be in Act 2 of Pinter's *The Caretaker* or in Willy Russell's *Shirley Valentine*, when Shirley talks to the wall.
2. Try writing a page of monologue in which the speaker addresses a listener. The listener must never speak, but

your monologue text has to hint at exactly who that listener is.

3. Try writing a verse of a poem for performance: give it a dimension of repetition: create a line that is repeated. A good source to look at as an example is work by The Joeys (see Paul Beasley's book, *Hearsay*, in the bibliography).

Study tips

1. When writing a piece for drama, speak everything aloud, try to live the parts. This is how Bruce Robinson, creator of *Withnail and I*, always work. (You need a quiet place for this).

2. Listen to a radio play on tape and have the text to read as you listen Compare the directions in italics with the actual voice realisations.

3. Try to create characters for dramatic projection by drawing a rough sketch, over-exaggerating all their clothes. When you come to write, these details will kick-start the more personality-based features of the person

****

Glossary of Terms

These terms are used briefly in this book. Here we offer a little more explanation, and the chapter numbers in which they appear are also given, unless a term is used repeatedly throughout.

catharsis	An unloading of an excess of emotion.
cinquain	A syllabic poem with five lines and a syllable count of 2/4/6/8/2 (Chapter 4).
critiquing	The stage in writing at which we are aware of our technique, verbal patterning and 'manufactured' style (Chapter 1).
defamiliarise	To create a sense of seeing something from an unusual perspective (Chapter 2).
discursive prose	Writing dealing with reflection, quasi-factual subjects and opinion or debate (Chapter 8).
documenting	The stage in writing at which we tend to list, describe and account for experience, without audience awareness (Chapter 1).
englyn	A syllabic poem with four lines, totalling 30 syllables (Chapter 4).
formalism	A view of writing stressing its 'literariness' and it condition of being a fabricated construct (Chapter 2).
free verse	Poetry arranged without any set formal patterning (Chapter 4).
genre	A defined category of writing with its own forms and conventions, such as science fiction, thrillers or romance.
genre cocktail	A mixture of genre styles (Chapter 1).
haiku	A syllabic poem of three lines with a count of 7/7/5 (Chapter 4).

metaphor	A use of words that describes or conveys meaning about one thing by means of a non-literal expression: *The room was no more than a shred of ripped cloth from the fabric of his life.*
metre	Versification: the patternings of stressed and unstressed syllables in formal poetry (Chapter 4).
narrating	The stage in writing at which we begin to tell stories or give accounts of experience, but at first without a directed style or specified reader (Chapter 1).
person	In narrative, the term used for the type of narrator and stance of narration (first, second and third *person*) (Chapter 9).
releasing	The stage in writing at which we 'unload' experience in order to understand its nature (Chapter 1).
simile	A comparison of the quality of one thing or concept with another, using 'like' or 'as': *He ran like the wind* (Chapter 2).
stanza	A section of a poem, usually in a set and repeated form (from the Italian for 'room') (Chapter 4).
syntax	The nature of word order and positioning of grammatical units in composition.
tanka	A syllabic poem with five lines, the count being 5/7/5/7/7 (Chapter 4).
template text	Writing that offers accessible possibilities for copying an aspect of style or form, such as a sonnet or a free verse poem with a 'visible' overt treatment of the subject (Chapter 1).
tripartite	Having three stages of composition or form.

113

Reference – Print

This list combines recommended works with writing referred to in the text.

1.   Reference Books

The Writers' and Artists' Yearbook (A and C Black) annual

Barry Turner, *The Writer's Handbook*(Macmillan) annual

2.   General

Paul Beasley, *Hearsay* (Red Fox) 1994

Renni Browne and Dave King, *Self-Editing for Fiction Writers* (Harper Collins) 2001

Sandy Brownjohn, *The Poet's Craft* (Hodder and Stoughton) 2002

Erich Fromm, *To Have or to be?* (Abacus) 1978

Natalie Goldberg, *Writing Down the Bones* (Shambhala) 1986

Jack Heffron, *The Writer's Idea Book* (Writers' Digest) 2000

Ann Hoffman, *Research for Writers* (A and C Black) 2001

Nicki Jackowska, *Write for Life* (Element) 1997

Ursula K. Le Guin, *Steering the Craft* (Eighth Mountain Press) 1998

John Lennard, *The Poetry Handbook* (OUP) 1996

Greg Light, 'Conceiving Creative Writing in Higher Education' in *Proceedings* of the Extending the Professional Writer Project (Sheffield Hallam University) 1999 pp. 37-50

David Mills, *Writing in Action* (Routledge) 1996

Neil Nixon, *Creative Writing* (Pocket Essentials) 2002

Josip Novakovitch, *Writing fiction Step by Step* (Story press) 1998

George Orwell, 'Why I Write' in *Decline of the English Murder and other Essays* (Penguin) 1975 pp. 180-188

Suzanna Ruthven, *Creative Pathways* (Alphard) 2002

Susan Sellers (ed) *Taking Reality by Surprise* (Women's Press) 1991

Stephen Wade, *WordShops* (Alphard) 2003

Nigel Watts, *Writing a Novel* (Hodder and Stoughton) 2003

Stella Whitelaw, *How to Write Short Stories* (Allison and Busby)

Jack Zipes, *Creative Storytelling* (Routledge) 1995

3.   Magazines

The New Writer P O Box 60, Cranbrook, Kent, TN17 2ZR

Writers' Forum P O Box 3229, Bournemouth, Dorset, BH1 1ZS

The Writer see the web site writermag. com

Note: there are far more magazines in the USA aimed at new writers, and many of the literary publications feature writing topics for all categories. There are far too many to list, but they can be found via Barnes and Noble web site and education programs.

Web-sites for Writers

This is only a select list, and many more may be found for poetry in Richard Cochrane's *Studying Poetry* (Studymates) 2000. Web sites for writing tend to be ephemeral, and the best advice is to be selective. But perhaps two categories are most useful to a new writer: the magazine and information sites that encourage writing for hypertext, and the ones devoted to a specific skill. For this list we are indebted to *Writers' forum* and to *The Writer's Handbook,* but I have added some of our favourites. For a more substantial list, and for up-dates, always check listings in the writing magazines.

Organisations: general
www.Sndc.demon.co.uk/als.htm   (Alliance of Literary Societies)

www.artscouncil.org.uk The Arts Council site. This is useful for details of grants, bursaries and events in support of new writing.

www.agentsassoc.co.uk The agents' site.

www.bbcco.uk The BBC site for access to all sites. This is valuable as a source of up-dates for BBC new writing initiatives, and gives advice on submission of work..

www.Britishcouncil.org

www.thecwa.co.uk For crime writing information.

www.eclectics.com/writing/writer Html. This offers advice on formats and technique.

www.ingenta.com This is your site if you need research help, and particularly if you are a non-fiction writer.

www.nawe.co.uk The site of the National Association of Writers in Education.

www.new-writers-consultancy.com Advice and appraisal for new writers.

www.societyofauthors.org invaluable for all professional advice and support.

Many new writers aim to join this Society, as soon as they start to be published.

www.trace.ntu.ac.uk This is the creative writing magazine and site of Nottingham Trent university, and comes highly recommended for new writers.

Resources and support for new writers

These sites and many more offer a range of resources and materials, such as tuition, focus on skills, publishing news, competitions and call for contributions. Many also have schemes for new writers to submit work within the category dealt with by a particular society of authors. The Romantic Novelists Association, for instance, has an annual submission scheme. Works are usually read by professional writers and critics.

www.YourDictionary.com
www.wordshops.co.uk
www.writersbbs.com
www.thewritersmind.com
www.absolutewrite.com
www.firstwriter.com
www.rna-uk.com
www.kate-walker.com
www.writingcorner.com
www.wordup.com
www.biscuitpublishing.com
www.thenewwriter.com

The best advice is to limit your time spent reviewing all these and select the most comprehensive, and then the one with your specific interests most prominently featured. Otherwise, surfing can replace valuable writing time.

Work Book for *Being a Professional Writer*

Lesson one

Phase one: What skills do I have and what do I need?

Writers need to find out exactly what they have as tools at the beginning of their writing careers. It doesn't matter what stage in your life you choose to take writing seriously. The point is that you want to find out w*hat* and *if* you can writer. The *if* is a small word with a massive protective barrier. It seems to guard those who have succeeded – keep them in a safe enclosure where the *real* writers live and find sustenance. They have proved they can write, people say. But is there a special formula that can be acquired in order that you may join the successful? Obviously not. But this is a list to start from: write some lists under these headings.

1. Your life-experience
2. Your certificated worth as a language-user
3. Your everyday encounters with words
4. Your reading or viewing

Phase two

Now take each topic and look closer. You will be amazed at the potential in each of these areas of imaginative resources.

Life experience: Text: Read the extract from *Villains and Enemies* at the back of the folder.

Obviously, not everyone is capable of being a constant observer of life. The idea of inspiration (whatever that is) suddenly striking you like a thunderbolt may still be current in some contexts, but the first step as a beginner, needing self-knowledge, is to consider the degree to which you relate to and feel a sense of placement in, life-experience. Questions to ask are these:

* Do you take an interest in other people's lives?
* How often have you tried to talk to people about their work?

* Do you enjoy reading/watching impressions of life similar to yours?
* would you agree that everyone has a story to tell? (Yours is?) Are you able to list at least three incidents from your life which are 'material'? Material can mean any angle you wish to place on one incident. Start with one specific event or experience, then write around the sensual and visual data that surround the moment.

e.g. Beach....man on horse riding by...I played, making a sandcastle...he had only one eye...called me little champion...I call him Young Lochinvar...from my favourite poem at school...one eye but beautiful. Made a drawbridge for the castle...he could ride in to safety.

Write a similar 'moment capture' and notes on your questions to yourself, for next time. The aim is to keep detail out of the picture at this point, and simply note the outline features of specific experience.

Lesson 2

Phase one Breaking Moulds

Topic: The most frustrating element in writing – of any kind – is often that you intend to produce something fresh, original, a new way of looking at a subject, and then, on paper, the result is too familiar or it lacks life, and so on.

One approach to escape this straightjacket is to use an unusual viewpoint or play with several viewpoints.

Examples for discussion:

1. *The man working on the roof caught sight of the woman out of the corner of his eye. At first it was just a flash of white he was aware of; then he instinctively turned to look across, and it was then he saw her body astride the fence, a red patch growing stealthily in the centre of her blouse.*

2. *The sound of footsteps on the asphalt should have been familiar but was not. They were not Jim's steps. It wasn't time for him to come home, either. She could have looked, but her contact-lenses were off, snugly in the case by her bedside.*

3. *The tiny parcel of clothes in the heart of the forest was slammed and kicked by the wind. Nature had it s future in her hands. Limbs wriggled, lungs screamed for help, just to be noticed by someone or something, but there was no pity in that raging storm.*

Phase two

Defamiliarisation

Victor Shklovsky – 'Habitualisation devours works, furniture, one's wife, and the fear of war...And art exists that one may recover the sensation of life; it exists to make one feel things, to make the stony STONY. The purpose of art is to impart the sensation of things as they are perceived and not as they are known.

Exercise: Take the following scene to be used at the opening of a story or novel. You should create a viewpoint that is so different from the norm that we see the scene as somehow strange to us as we read.

As the story begins, there is a man at the wheel of a car. The car is parked in a lay-by in the country. Three police officers are observing the man. They are nervous. They carry firearms. Help is on the way. The road is an arterial route; constant traffic, bright summer day.

You might choose to 'show' the scene in the way that a pilot, an animal, a schoolchild etc. might see it. Or you could make the story emerge as internal thoughts of someone.

<u>Lesson 3</u>
Genres and genre cocktail <u>Use the Conventions</u>
The first stage of this session is to read together some openings from genre fiction. The class should bring in a selection, reflecting a range of interests.
Discussion points;
What is genre?
What language uses give clues about the intended genre of a piece?
Can genre writing be as effective as 'serious' fiction as a social commentary or as philosophic, reflective writing?

The group should work around the definition that genre uses a set of accepted codes and conventions which reflect a norm of writing technique. Texts which do not fit easily into genres could be discussed e.g. *Kes, Tom Jones, Oranges are Not the only Fruit etc.*
These definitions provide a useful launching-pad:
'Genre should be conceived, we think, as a grouping of literary works based, theoretically, upon both an outer and an inner form (attitude, tone, purpose- more crudely, subject and audience'). Rene Welleck *Theory of Literature.*

Art develops further until a form is achieved and valued for its own sake. The achievement of form is signalled by a revolution in the ordering of the constituent parts. Elder Olson *An Outline of Poetic Theory*.

Genre cocktails:

The writing exercise for this session is to work on a genre cocktail – a mixture of genre techniques to create a new one. For example, you might interlink a detective narrative with a science fiction, as in the film *Blade runner*. Or, discuss and comment on this passage which mixes Philip Marlowe with the gritty northern realism of Barstow or Priestley:

As I approached the door of my office on the third floor of the Ebenezer Sykes building in Crapley, I knew there was a dame waiting for me – and a dangerous one at that. The perfume lingered on the landing, just beneath the painting of Ebenezer himself, hands in waistcoat pocket, looking complacent.

I tilted my flat cap, put the pipe away, still warm, into my Gannex mac pocket, arranged the false smile, and peered around the door. She was blonde, young and lethal. Her legs went right up to where a man should never look, but I looked anyway. It was a day for risks. I'd already brought the *Telegraph* and spat into gutter. I was mean as a lawyer without a brief and the world was going to know it.

'Hi, fella…you Bill Sidebottom, private Dick?'

'I could be lass, but steady on, I'm feelin' a bit parky. I'll just put this gasfire on, then I'm all yours, flower…'

Lesson 4

Dialogue   All Talk?

In narrative, dialogue can serve several functions:

1.   To inform the reader about a character's personality, habits, background etc.

2.   To add to descriptive detail.

3.   To give essential factual information in an interesting way.

4.   To add variety and interest – it usually gives a sense of realism very quickly.

Consider the following and compare them. Each extract comes from the opening of each text. Ask yourself what the notion of 'authentic' dialogue means and what it demands of the writer.

1.   After the deluge of sound ceased, after the wind passed, the sailor fell, was sick. They were in a desert of air.

'Goddam! get me out of this,' the sailor shouted.

'Stand up,' the little man said; he began to pull. Crunching sounds came up.

'It's ice' the sailor said. 'Get me out of this.' Falling again, hands became feelers, pawing about. 'I know ice' he said, 'something always moving under ice, I know.'

(James Hanley: *No Directions*)

2.   'All the time the wind was south-west you were deadly keen on seals.'

'Was I?' Allen idly stopped fumbling in the pocket of his coat, then asked with interest: 'Been seeing your friend the boatman again?'

'Yes. Why?'

'This meterological knowledge'.

'I suppose you think I'm incapable of noticing anything for myself'.

'No.'

(Christopher Isherwood *All the Conspirators*)

3.   'Something a little strange, that's what you notice, that she's not a woman like all the others. She looks fairly young, twenty-five maybe – or a little more, petite face, a little catlike, small turned-up nose. The shape of her face, it's…more roundish than oval, broad forehead,

pronounced cheeks too but then they come down to a point, like with cats.'

'What about her eyes?'

'Clear, pretty sure they're green, half-closed to focus better on the drawing. She looks at her subject: the black panther at the zoo, which was quiet at first, stretched out in its cage.' (Manuel Puig: *Kiss of the Spider-Woman*)

Exercises

1. Write an opening of a story entirely in dialogue, with the speakers discussing something which will clearly show their different personalities.

2. Select the opening page of dialogue at the beginning of a play, then convert this into prose, including all the information, including a description of the scene.

3. Write a short dialogue in which you introduce a specific fact – a statistic or historical information. Make it dramatically interesting.

   Note that one fact alone can be of sufficient interest, given the right dramatic situation, emotional velocity, and so on. Every fact does not need to be immediately and deeply relevant to characters, either.

Lesson 5
Writing Monologue <u>Reading Insignificance?</u>
The monologue is perhaps most associated with the art-narrative rather than the popular narrative; that is to say, as a monologue conveys the inner thoughts of a character in an apparently disjointed and digressive way, the reader has to be patient, prepared to accept that to read such narratives is to follow the vagaries of the human mind, in order to achieve something about some universal knowledge of human traits. The great set-pieces of Absurd theatre, such as the close of Act Two of Pinter's *The Caretaker*, or the intensely realistic method of Alan Bennett's much-acclaimed *Talking Heads,* show the strengths of this writing as a method of revealing psychological depths.

There are some issues which are worth considering, though, from the sheer 'mechanics' of writing such styles:

- Is it always possible to make the apparently trivial into 'a great theme'?
- Can interest be sustained by following the ramblings of actual inner thoughts?
- Does a monologue have to have an element of artifice, or could a real piece of 'speech' written directly from inner thoughts be 'shaped' naturally?

How is variety included? Usually by location and other people etc. There are wider stylistic issues to consider also, but the fundamental issue is how to create interest, tension and so on. In other words, is a convincing 'voice' enough to succeed in this form?

Exercises
1. Read the following extracts from monologues and suggest ways in which the storyline could be changed or developed in order to add more depth or more social commentary.

125

a) *I was waiting by the bus-stop...the one I'd been standing at for the last God knows how many years...well, this young man had been there, and these two older fold – a man of about fifty and a woman (very smartly dressed) of about, oh, I'd say maybe forty. Well, I'd never said this before cos we hardly ever spoke...in fact never. Only nodded like. Well, this particular morning I said, a bit nervously, 'Mornin'', and do you know, their heads turned in shock. The older man actually said to me, 'Do I know you?' That's what he said. Not a word of lie. 'Do I know you!' Don't that just take the biscuit? That's England for you...*

b) *Don't know why I wait here every week for him. He don't care one flea, not a maggot. In fact, do I need the feller in me life? I sometimes wonder. I mean, he'll be round that corner any minute now, frown on his face, miserable as sin, pretending he's not going to touch me for a few quid. For the ruddy horses that is. His beloved nags. He loves 'em more than me...anybody could see that. But the worm is going to turn, oh yes my lad. Yes me bonny lad. No more easy peezy Sheila in your life. Just you come round there smiling and I might let you off, but I know you're gonna look like a wet Sunday in Bradford.*

2. Write a monologue based on one of the following storylines. Write the opening page.

a) A young woman has left a huge city, packed a suitcase quickly and caught a coach north. She is wrecked by stress, and wants to escape a street of crime, noise and hellish brutality. Next to her is a young man with a walkman plugged into his ears. Write her thoughts as she looks around and wonders whether to speak...

b) A man of about twenty-five is walking across town to visit his brother. But this is no ordinary visit. He is deeply in debt after embezzling funds from the Working Men's Club of which he is secretary. He has gambled away thousands of pounds. His younger brother is the only person he knows who has the funds to bale him out. But they haven't spoken for at least two years…just exchanged polite Christmas cards. Pay a visit to his head and inner thought.

Further reading: Alan   Bennett   *Talking   Heads*   BBC 1988

Robert Browning   *Men and Women*   Dent Everyman ed.   1975
Roger Karshner   *Working Class Monologues* Dramaline   1988

See also audition books for actors which contain a wide variety of monologue forms.

Lesson 6
Factual Writing   <u>Categories and Audiences</u>

We now begin the introductory level workshops on writing with a factual basis. This could incorporate any of these forms and conventions:
documentary
feature
instructional
interview/profile
review
opinion/argument/polemic

The approach is not the first consideration; the first step is to consider the process involved in any writing with a factual element and therefore also with an objective which is to inform the reader. Originality is not an essential component either. As Dr Johnson said, 'Men more often need to be reminded than informed.' That is, there is always a market for short, informative essays and articles which give important information. The general process will be as follows:
Stage 1.   Consider aims and target reader
Stage 2.   Research the subject well
Stage 3.   Write up notes into a structured piece
The *aims* will obviously relate to such purposes as whether you wish to put statement of facts before entertainment, humour, tone and so on. In other words, are you primarily out to persuade, to instruct or to entertain with the facts you have collected? Is the aim to mix some or all of these? Here is a useful exercise to consider some of these things.
You are to write an article for the complete beginner in a subject that you know very well. Choose a hobby or leisure interest for this. Then write a list of what purposes the article might have. Express this in verbs. E.g. To remind, to advise, to recommend, to condemn etc.

Now, select just one of these verbs and write your first paragraph in line with the main intention. For instance, here is an example on the subject of 'Getting into classical Music' for a general hobbies magazine aimed at young people.

So you maybe never even wondered what a conductor needs to know to use a baton, or whether Mozart really did write the Requiem from a mysterious caller? Maybe you never thought a second about what classical music is all about than the need to tap your toes when hear the *William Tell Overture?* Well let me surprise you if you think this is typical of people under twenty. This year's Prom concert's famous Last Night enticed 25,000 people into the Albert Hall who were under the age of twenty. Rap and Jungle are not the only musical forms around.

Your research notes for any projected article should use these headings:

Topic   Style   Outlet
          Readership/audience

Your writer's log should note preparatory reading in your selected specialist area. For instance, supposing you want to write a piece on school bullying and you have done some interviews and research reading. You have your rough notes ready. What do you do in order to decide on where your submission will go? Use the above headings and read all the education pages of the daily nations, the weekly magazines and the specialist publications aimed at teachers. The range of tones and styles will tell you where your best chance of success lies.

Exercise

Choose a specific topic within the subject area of people returning to learn and research the market. Write notes on the potential market for a specified article. Bring your notes to the next session if you are working on a course.

Lesson 7
Textless Histories   From Interview to Article

To set up as a freelance feature/factual writer you could choose to specialise in writing based on interviews and profiles. There is so much 'material' in the lives of people – ordinary or extraordinary. The Oral History movement has been one aspect of this, with historians realising that articulate people of advance age can be a kind of 'living history', but in a more journalistic sense, it has to be said that each of us has a story to tell.

Even if you know no shorthand, you can work with a notebook, micro-recorder and typewriter or PC and produce articles about people's lives quite easily, yet in a variety of styles. Consider this example.

Stage one: You find out from a local newspaper that a man is writing his memoirs of the Second World War. Contact him and arrange an interview. Do some market research as to national outlets who would use an article on the anniversary of a battle or, obviously, on Remembrance Day.

Stage two: Use the micro-recorder to have all the words spoken, but put essential headings in your notebook.

Stage three: At your desk, plug in the earphones and play the interview. Write the statements worthy to be used and keep the finger on the pause button!

Stage four: Write up the article.

Of course, this type of writing can cover local magazines and newspapers, right up to specialist publications. The way to make all this easy on yourself is to limit your range, decide on a subject area, then do these practical record and monitoring methods:

Keep cuttings in a file – topics in your subject range.

In an index book (or on disk) keep and update a list of editors and addresses.

In a notebook or in a computer file, keep transcripts or summaries of all

interviews done. Many could be used later for a different outlet.

Interviewing tips:

Write questions which demand full answers. Begin with 'How far do you

think...?' and 'Why do you think...?'

Do research on the background of the topic before you begin.

Keep eye contact with the subject and look responsive and attentive.

Set a time limit and keep the subject relevant – but be polite in doing this.

Exercise

The class first has to *decide on a new publication* on current/social affairs. They act as an editorial board and decide what contributions they wish to invite. A simplified stylesheet could be produced and discussed.

A stylesheet could be written with these headings:

1. Target readership.
2. Degree of formality in the vocabulary and syntax.
3. Length and variety of sentences.
4. Use of pronouns and extent of quotation.

Interview your neighbour in the class on a chosen topic. Some suggestions are: their experience of school; involvement in leisure/charity work/cultural events etc.

Write and ask about ten questions. Then exchange roles.

From your rough notes, write an opening paragraph for the publication and stylesheet decided on by the class.

Some opening techniques to practise

These are some effective ways to begin a factual article

1. A question.
   e.g. *Have you ever considered what goes through your mind when you're a copper on the beat at here in the morning?*
2. Quote from subject:
   e.g. *'I like to think about the family...or my stamp collection...it kills time', Constable Smith tells me.*
3. Quote from a well known source:
   'A policeman's lot is not a happy one.' W.S. Gilbert said.
4. Image:
   Plodding on the beat in the early hours can seem like a guided tour of eternity.
5. Hyperbole:
   The dogs of Hell can be let loose in Hull at one in the morning when the drunks start fighting each other, as Constable Smith knows well.
   Additional reading:
   Joan Clayton *Interviewing for Journalists* Piatkus
   John Hines *The Way to Write Magazine Articles* Elm Tree Books
   Ann Hoffmann *Research for Writers* OUP

Lesson 8
Witness to...?   <u>I was there!</u>

The word 'documentary' has suggestions of logging, monitoring some kind of detail, some actuality which will reflect the truth. The modern television documentary or the traditional documentary film means, for most people, a prying into life 'as it is lived'. A useful way to approach this is to consider the idea of a witness to some event. This is the topic for this workshop.

The notion of witnessing something can apply to a significant event, such as a person who saw a landmark trade union strike or a murder, but it can also be simply social history, such as a midwife in the 1940s who can say interesting things about her professional life before the emergence of the modern medical technology we all take for granted.

These are some possibilities for the potential 'recipe' to include in documentary writing:

- Dramatic, intense first-person accounts
- Straight historical data
- Letters, journals, diaries etc.
- Statistics

Notice that these imply a specific way of handling information, depending on your target audience or purpose. Suppose, for example, you want to write an article based on some statistics about education. You find some basic statistics about a local further education college, such as the fact that maybe very few people from ethnic minorities attend. Access courses (courses equivalent to 'A' level for mature students). You discover that over the last ten years, only 2% of students on these courses have been from such minority groups.

What possible documentary treatments of the subject are possible? You could find students who are attending language classes locally and talk to them. Find the cultural, social and religious reasons why they do not go to Access courses. Or you could relate the local facts to national trends. The find potential markets in the press or in educational magazines.

What does documentary style mean?

A famous definition from John Grierson, the founder of the British documentary film, is the 'imaginative interpretation of actuality'. Here is an approach that means taking people doing or saying interesting things about human experience and letting them speak for themselves – but not totally. You edit, select and arrange what they say by providing a commentary for the reader.

Exercise

Choose an occupation which is unusual – one that you know very little about and write a list of questions you would ask a person who does that job (e.g. undertaker, novelist, advertising agency work etc.). Direct your questions towards a particular 'angle' on that job such as sensation, curiosity, humour, sarcasm and so on. Then write an article on *imagined* answers. In other words, it could read almost like fiction.

After that, try out the real thing. Arrange an interview with such a person and try the approach and viewpoint. The difference between the two versions will highlight what real documentary writing is about.

Further study and practice:
a) Find articles in the *New Statesman* weekly which are concerned with documentary investigation. List the styles/techniques used to give a sense of realism and actuality.
b) Add this to a checklist of how the material has been *interpreted* for the reader.

Further reading:
Christopher Dobson   *The Freelance Journalist*   Butterworth Heinemann
Paul Mills *Writing in Action* Routledge

Lesson 9 Introducing... <u>Your Guide To</u>

A particularly useful and manageable form to write in when starting out as a factual writer is the informative guide to any subject you care to mention. People do not seem to mind reading about Feng Shui, wine or American Football for the twentieth time. There are some things in life which always seem to provoke curiosity, and we like to be informed.

Consider the various ways of putting across information on any subject.

1.   The facts. Literal, direct and relying on statistics etc.
2.   A personal angle. The day you tried to understand chess or squash and went to learn.
3.   The A-Z guide. Here you can present established facts, sourced from a reference book or from an expert, in a chatty, readable way.
4.   You interview the expert and take things words for word.

Each approach has its own advantages, of course. But before you practise these and decide which suits you best, let's have a look at some short examples of what not to do when it comes to presenting facts: these are extracts from a range of articles. Note down what you feel is the weakness in each case.

1.   Photography is an expensive mistress. Devote your time to her and you will be forever haunting shops and drooling over the gear you can't afford. You will buy every glossy magazine you see, and imagine yourself as a millionaire, stocking up on the latest models of automatic cameras. But it need not be like this. You need to decide early on what is *your* type of photography and stick to what is needed. You might need a lightmeter, a fish-eye lens, a cable release. Who know?

135

2. Consider all the facts you need at your fingertips to take up a small business. Just think of the contracts you will need. The experts, the experienced. Where will you find them, and can you trust them? Have you realised how important such things are? But you have started to read this, having bought this magazine, and that is a bright start.

3. Body-building need not require a massive investment in equipment. You do not have to re-vamp your garage and turn it into a gym. There are other ways of getting fit. But spend a while simply assessing your needs as you aspire to a peak of physical rightness. You need to be attuned to your body, to eat properly, to somehow see your body as a machine and as a spiritual, individual organ, part of you, your self, your being-in-the-world. Then turn thoughts to muscle structure and blood pressure, body mass ad heart-rate.

Maybe (1) is fine until the last mind-boggling sentence? (2) is disorganised. The reader would be confused all the way here. (3) Commits the sin of bombarding with jargon.

Exercise

The secret of this kind of writing is to plan and structure well before you write. Try this short exercise. Imagine that you are writing a handbook on a subject you know well. Decide on the chapter headings and list these, then write a checklist of the information that a beginner would need, in order of importance, as a basis for a first, introductory chapter. Your rationale for this should be based on a sensible and user-friendly breakdown of the material you intend to cover, staged for progressive use, with recaps of factual information.

Lesson 10
Reviewing the Situation A Form Open to All?

In theory, anyone could sit down and write a review, providing that he or she has a basic ability to express ideas and responses clearly and with interest. We all must have taken part in a discussion about a book, a play or a film and then realised that someone made us see things another way, opened up other avenues of understanding about art.

But things are not so simple. To write a review of a text in a set number of words is a challenge to a writer which entails a specific set of disciplines. A cursory reading of *The Writer's Handbook* would perhaps give the impression that magazines and journals are always looking out for freelance reviews, but this is not so uncomplicated as it may seem. However, a constructive first step is to consider what the function of a review is. (I will use book reviews in my examples, for the sake of ease and consistency):

- To inform the reader about value
- To give an educated opinion about style and content
- To introduce readers to a quality writer
- To enthuse about a personal favourite
  It might seem that a review is a personal indulgence – a chance to express the

Reviewer's opinions and taste. Yet, a proper reading of the books pages in Sunday supplements should make it clear that a good review does several useful things. It can give compact information about the author, highlight the strengths of a style, indicate what additions to existing knowledge are in the text, and so on. Having said this, it is still possible to allow a reviewer space to indulge personal, highly individuated readings, but these are rare.

The length is also a crucial factor. Imagine the constraints on the writer who is asked to review a detailed, academic work in only 300 words. Equally, journals such as *The Times Literary Supplement* may sometimes allow a length of 3,000 words if the subject is deemed to be significant enough.

With these aspects of the craft in mind, what are the essential requirements in style and treatment of the subject? Here are some suggestions:

1.   Knowledge – based on close reading or on the wider context.
2.   Personal experience. For instance, in most cases, the reviewer has relevant experience which lends some depth to the writing.
3.   Related publications. Obviously, editors like specialist to review in most cases.
4.   Entertainment with information. It should be, above all else, *readable*. Potentially, a review is a mini-essay, with weight in its own right. The writer can easily provide an interpretation of a book's central argument or plot.

Examples of approaches:

Here are some common approaches to the problem of how to review.

The authoritarian – I know more than the writer. My review will make this clear to all my readers.

The dilettante -   I am not an expert as the author is, and sheer energy and gushing praise will fill the page well enough.

The sceptic -   Do we really need another book on Dickens? There's nothing worth writing about here. Try again. Maybe I could do better, but I have better things to do.

The sceptic -   I shall weigh and consider, perhaps confusing you even more with the weight of my learning. But by God, you will feel that you have learned something.

Exercise

Write notes on the effectiveness of these styles to reviewing. Which would you find most appealing to the general reader. Assume these are all from weekly newspapers covering books for non-specialists.

Novels like this are rare as white rhinos. And when you do find such a treasure, enjoy it, relish it, take your time. I was sorry to reach the last page of this adventure yarn – a tale well in the tradition of Kipling or Rider Haggard.

If you like your stories plain and direct – and actually about something you can recognise as real life, then stay away from this novel. You will feel a numbness in the brain after three pages. No help is offered, and you cry out for footnotes or even translations at times.

The author's three previous books dealt with the northern states of Italy in the Renaissance. This makes a new departure, but the themes are still there – loss, parting and isolation in woman's lot. But the Feminism is only there in the people and the dialogue, never thrust at you like an essential therapy to cure your narrow mind.

Lesson 11

The Studymates book is organised into workshops covering both factual and fictional writing, but now the material is more demanding, ambitious and innovative. The aim now is to give full rein to your own skills and natural tastes in language use. Much of the material here relates to subjects which are often discussed in specialist short courses, but again, I want to simply introduce a range of approaches.

After completing the workshops at the introductory level, you should have some idea now of what style, genre and format suits your talents and aims and therefore you could concentrate on the topics at advanced level which relate to work already done.

Before starting this next stage, however, it will pay to consider once more the points about each individual writer's aims. Do you have more idea now about your potential expertise, your necessary decisions about what to write and why? These questions are worth some thought at this point:

1. Does 'getting into print' seem to be a priority for you, or does learning skills matter more, regardless of time available?

2. Do you feel confident enough to submit a piece of writing to an editor now?

   Think about the reasons behind your answer.

3. Have you read consistently in the area in which you want to publish – and therefore do you feel confident that you 'know the market' as well as knowing the style, conventions, and so on?

4. have you considered reading your work to anyone for a constructive criticism, before submitting it for publication?

5. Do you feel fully aware of what re-reading and editing involves?

If any of these questions are impossible to answer, then check in the A-Z of technique at the end of the folder. It is all really a case of knowing which tasks are essential and which are optional. The fact is that authors now are asked to do quite a lot of work previously done by publishers, and this means that as a writer, you need more skills than simply writing sentences and building up to novels or biographies.

Lesson 12
Making an impression <u>More than one way to...</u>

The easiest habit to acquire in writing fiction is to give the facts of a scene or person just as they appear to the eye. This can be effective, of course, and simplicity often presents something to the reader that is becoming less easy to find in the current climate of experimental writing. But what the Impressionist painters did for landscape you can do for your fictional world – with some practice. Reflect on these descriptions:

1. On the pillion, John felt the air whipping at his ears as Gray pushed the machine on to the ton. They were tearing up Beacroft Hill like bullets. John's heart was in his mouth. But he daren't say a word. Gray yelled and screamed with the joy of it. John gritted his teeth and tried to keep his dinner in his belly.

2. Cold air lashing the ears. A grinding, churning rumble underneath between his legs. John shook with a nameless fear. The road came up to meet his gaping wonder as the tinny, rattling plates of metal around that thrumming engine pulsed excitement into his veins.

The first only differs significantly from the second in that it is more distant, less concerned with the actual sensations of experiencing the bike ride. The reader sees John as in a documentary, in a sense, observing all details as they are drawn and examined. The second is impressionistic, in that the reader feels the sensations more directly. The writer needs to find words to describe the feelings, sensual responses and visual shapings of the experience itself.

For this reason, impressionistic writing often makes use of some useful techniques:

- Using sentences without subjects
- Cutting out explanatory adverbs and adjectives where needed
- Positioning the reader so that one angle of view or feeling is given

In other words, the aim is to make explanation minimal. Consider six things which could be said about a building. It could be tall, brown, old, without windows, on a hill and exposed to the noise of a nearby motorway. You could give all these details in the orthodox way, building the information gradually to 'set the scene' like an establishing shot in a film. Or, with a sense of perspective, you could present just one angle to the reader. Maybe something like this:

You felt dizzy squinting to look up to the heights of the windowless block of stone: dizzy because something about the plod up the crumbling steps made you want to keep an eye on what was above, feeling like a warrior expecting a defence of the walls he was about to storm.

This simply misses out a large amount of normal description and expected data. It also places the reader in a position which demands thought and adjustment, seeing the narrative from a viewpoint which asks for some attention and challenges a few stereotypes of descriptive writing.

All that is needed is some thought about the ways in which the best impressionistic writers go to work. Some interesting examples are provided by the short stories of Katherine Mansfield and Anton Chekhov. In their stories, the reader often feels an immediate contact with the perspective needed. In Chekhov's story, *he Swedish Match,* for instance, we have:

The window had a gloomy, ominous air. It was covered by a faded green curtain. One corner of the curtain was slightly turned back, which made it possible to peep into the bedroom.

This is so simple, so minimal, yet it invites a view, a stance on the part of the reader.

Exercises
1. Try to write an interchange of dialogue in which the reader is made to feel a sense of 'overhearing' the talk.
2. Convey a scene by building on the effects of a storm or tempest, but seen from the point of view of something non-human.

****